The Mensa Book of Literary Quizzes

OTHER <u>MENSA</u> BOOKS BY ABBIE F. SALNY:

The Mensa Genius Quiz Book (with Marvin Grosswirth)
The Mensa Genius Quiz Book Two (with Marvin Grosswirth)
The Mensa Book of Words
The Mensa Think Smart Book (with Lewis Burke Frumkes)
The Mensa Quiz-a-Day Book

THE MENSA BOOK OF
Literary Quizzes

Abbie F. Salny

HarperPerennial
A Division of HarperCollinsPublishers

FIRST EDITION

Designed by Joan Greenfield

Library of Congress Cataloging-in-Publication Data

Salny, Abbie F.
Mensa book of literary quizzes/by Abbie Salny.—1st HarperPerennial ed.
p.   cm.
ISBN 0-06-096535-5 (paper)
1. Literature—Examinations, questions, etc.   2. Literary recreations.   I. Title.
PN43.S34   1991
807.6—dc20   90-56096

91 92 93 94 95 DT/FG 10 9 8 7 6 5 4 3 2 1

*As always, and forever, to Jerry,
and to my dear mother for helping me grow up literate*

C O N T E N T S

The Mensa Book of Literary Quizzes

INTRODUCTION

There has been a rush, even a spate, of books lately about cultural literacy: Do you know what you are supposed to know? Are you culturally literate? Such books are excellent for checking on your general knowledge (and for giving you a guilt trip), but this book is not intended to do that. The book is designed so that you can have fun while checking your literary knowledge of facts, odd facts, and miscellanea. All of the quizzes, games, puzzles, and other forms of literary amusement have been chosen with a steady eye on one factor—most of the material is in the conscious or unconscious repertoire of people who read. (If you are not a real reader, it is highly unlikely you will be buying this book.)

The selections covered in the quizzes range from nursery rhymes to the King James version of the Bible; from fairy tales to Pulitzer Prize winners; from authors who published only one book—but that one an immortal classic like *Gone With the Wind*—to authors who have written dozens and, in the case of Isaac Asimov, hundreds of books. There is an excellent chance that you will know a large number of the selections, quotations, and authors. But will you be able to solve the matching puzzles or figure out the literary cryptograms or "drop-in quotes" or the matching pairs? This collection is designed to amuse, stimulate, and call for the famous psychological response known as the "Aha" reaction. It is not a book to be read through at one sitting. Treat it as you would a fine after-dinner Napoleon brandy and take it in small sips. This is a collection of tidbits to enjoy, to savor, to ponder, and to puzzle over.

Of course, we also hope that if you come across some long-forgotten work, or an author whom you once enjoyed, you'll go back and reread the book or the poem again. The scraps of memory you may now have can be turned into full-blown, accurate quotes if you do so, and "flash upon that inward eye that is the bliss of solitude."

The vague niggling sense of having forgotten something can be assuaged, and your ego massaged gently, by verifying the actual story for yourself.

In short, you can enjoy yourself on several levels. Take this as fun, pure and simple. Take it as an amusing test of your cultural literacy and your memory. Or take it as a refresher course in English (and a little foreign) literature. The choice is up to you, but you can do the quizzes on all levels. We've designed them that way.

And for all you puzzle fans who just like quizzes and puzzles, you don't really need to worry about any of that. Just enjoy the challenge of the puzzles, quizzes, and games.

Happy puzzling, good memory, and much enjoyment.

CHAPTER 1

Authors—Their Lives and Their Characters

I.
On the left is a brief description of some aspect of a famous author's life. Fill in the appropriate name on the blank line.

1. This nineteenth-century French author is considered one of the founders of the "problem" novel. Noted for stormy romances with other writers, and at least one world-famous musician, the author wrote under an assumed name. _____

2. This Scotsman suffered from tuberculosis most of his life. Despite this, he traveled widely with his American wife and finally settled in Samoa, where he died and is buried. _____

3. This nineteenth-century American author wrote both romantic and moralistic novels. The son of a ship captain, he worked in a customs house and also as a surveyor of the Salem, Massachusetts, port. _____

4. The first husband of this famous French writer of the early twentieth century kept her a virtual prisoner while she wrote the semiautobiographical novels that brought her fame (and the fortune he seems to have been worried about). A dress style was named for the heroine of her most famous book. _____

5. This nineteenth-century English author collaborated with Charles Dickens on a few short stories, but is best known as the author of the books considered the first genuine detective and mystery books. _____

6. A Romantic poet, he was expelled from Oxford for his defense of atheism. He married twice; his second wife, the daughter of a famous writer and radical and of a well-known early feminist, became famous in her own right. The author lived in poverty until he inherited a fortune from his grandfather. He drowned at the age of thirty, off the coast of Italy. _____

7. This prolific contemporary writer is noted for his long, detailed, immensely popular novels covering vast expanses of time and territory. His first collection of stories came out of his experiences in the Navy during World War II and has been adapted for the musical stage and movies. _____

8. This British writer traveled extensively in his job for the post office. His most famous novels centered around the social and clerical life of a cathedral town in Southern England. _____

9. This French writer, considered the greatest author of his generation, led a turbulent and active life. He wrote plays, poems, and criticism, as well as fiction, and also painted. _____

10. This Italian writer, who wrote in English, enjoyed a tremendous popularity during the 1920s. One of his heroes passed into the popular imagination as the image of the derring-do swashbuckler. _____

II.
Many famous authors have written under pen names. Real names are given on the left, pen names on the right. Match them.

1. François Marie Arouet
2. Frederick Van Rensselaer Dey
3. J. A. Wight
4. Marie H. Beyle
5. William Sydney Porter
6. Charlotte Brontë
7. John B. Wilson
8. Eric Blair
9. Erle Stanley Gardner
10. Manfred Lee and Frederick Dannay

a. James Herriot
b. Stendhal
c. Currer Bell
d. O. Henry
e. Voltaire
f. George Orwell
g. Nick Carter
h. Anthony Burgess
i. Ellery Queen
j. A. A. Fair

III.
The five names shown below are all, with one exception, the scrambled names of authors. Unscramble the names and find the "odd man out."

EMAWROL NSTOSNEEV SSNIIOR STEAK GNIPLKI

IV.
While the following cryptogram is not about a writer, it is about writing in general. This is a simple substitution cryptogram, in which the same letter replaces its match all the way through.
(Clue: the author is an American humorist.)

"JU UPPL NF GJGUFFO ZFBST UP EJTDPWFS UIBU J
IBE OP UBMFOU GPS XSJUJOH CVU J DVMEOU
HJWF JU VQ CFDBVTF CZ UIBU UJNF J XBT UPP
GBNPVT." CFODIMFZ

V.

Geoffrey Chaucer, a royal relative by marriage and a noted poet, the first major poet to write in the English vernacular, is most famous for his collection of Canterbury Tales, *a group of stories told by pilgrims on their way to Canterbury Cathedral. Name four of the more than a dozen characters who told their stories in this work.*

1. _____

2. _____

3. _____

4. _____

Chaucer also wrote many other popular and famous works. Give the titles of at least two.

1. _____

2. _____

VI.

The Pulitzer Prize, the most prestigious literary award in the United States, has been awarded most years since 1918. A list of Pulitzer Prize winners follows. Give the name of the book(s) for which they won the prize.

1. John Steinbeck, 1940 _____

2. Ernest Hemingway, 1953 _____

3. William Faulkner, 1955, 1963 _____

4. Margaret Mitchell, 1937 _____

5. John Updike, 1982, 1990 _____

6. James Agee, 1958 _____

7. Katherine Anne Porter, 1966 _____

8. Saul Bellow, 1976 _____

9. Allen Drury, 1960 _____

10. Harper Lee, 1961 _____

VII.

*The following word square contains, in no particular order, the
names of eight poets. If you start at the correct letter and move in
any direction you will find the last names. There is one
meaningless letter.*

E	E	T	K	E	L	L	A	W
B	N	O	R	A	I	M	Y	H
T	S	F	P	S	T	Y	T	I
O	L	O	S	S	E	E	M	A
H	M	E	E	H	L	L	N	X

VIII.

Samuel Pepys's Diary, *one of our best records of late-seventeenth-
century life, includes a description by an eyewitness of
the great fire of London. The* Diary *was
partially published in 1825. Why?
James Boswell's famous life of Dr. Samuel Johnson was also not
published for many years. Why?*

IX.

*At least two authors dreamed some of their most famous works.
Name two such authors and the famous works they dreamed up.
(One of the works is supposed to be opium inspired.)*

X.

Money, money, money. It is a subject of constant preoccupation for many people, including authors. The following quotes all concern money. Identify them by author or source.

1. Money answereth all things. _____

2. Ah, take the cash and let the credit go. _____

3. From birth to age eighteen, a girl needs good parents. From eighteen to thirty-five, she needs good looks. From thirty-five to fifty-five she needs a good personality. From fifty-five on, she needs good cash. _____

4. . . . he had started a story once that began, "The very rich are different from you and me." And how someone had said to Julian, "Yes, they have more money." _____

5. There is no road to wealth so easy and respectable as that of matrimony. _____

6. The almighty dollar, that great object of universal devotion throughout our land, seems to have no genuine devotees in these peculiar villages. _____

7. Give crowns, and pounds and guineas, But not your heart away. _____

8. And Mammon wins his way where seraphs might despair. _____

9. Love of money is the root of all evil. _____

10. That's the way the money goes, Pop goes the weasel! _____

XI.

Each of the following authors has one major factor in common, a fact that is rather unusual. Explain what they have in common—and the particular circumstances, for each author.

1. O. Henry   _____

2. Richard Lovelace _____

3. Leigh Hunt   _____

4. Victor Hugo   _____

5. John Bunyan   _____

6. François Villon   _____

7. Oscar Wilde   _____

8. Sir Thomas More   _____

9. André Chénier   _____

10. Emile Zola   _____

XII.

Imaginary countries have existed in the minds of authors since the beginning of recorded time. Match the following imaginary places— cities, countries, or wherever—with the appropriate author. Authors are listed on the right.

1. Shangri-La	a.	Samuel Butler
2. Utopia	b.	Horace Walpole
3. Erewhon	c.	James Hilton
4. Gopher Prairie	d.	Jonathan Swift
5. Barchester	e.	Sir Thomas More
6. Lilliput	f.	Anthony Trollope
7. La Mancha	g.	Anthony Hope
8. Brigadoon	h.	Alan Jay Lerner
9. Ruritania	i.	Cervantes
10. Serendip	j.	Sinclair Lewis

XIII.

Several presidents wrote books (or at least published books under their name) or extremely important documents. Some might be considered true literary successes, but these presidents were indeed literary figures. The names are on the left. Either their only work or their best-known work is on the right. Match the president and his writing.

1. Theodore Roosevelt

2. Thomas Jefferson

3. Thomas Woodrow Wilson

4. Richard M. Nixon

5. John Adams

6. Dwight David Eisenhower

7. Ulysses S. Grant

8. John Fitzgerald Kennedy

9. Herbert Hoover

10. James Madison

a. *The Federalist Papers*

b. *The Challenges We Face*

c. *Principles of Mining*

d. *At Ease*

e. *Winning of the West*

f. *A History of the American People*

g. Declaration of Independence

h. *Personal Memoirs*

i. *Profiles in Courage*

j. *The Diary and Autobiography of* _____

ANSWERS

I.

1. George Sand. This gifted lady, whose real name was Lucie Aurore Dupin (Amandine is sometimes given as her first name), was originally married to Baron Dudevant. She was a devoted mother to her two children, and took them with her in all her travels. She was friendly, but not romantically involved, with writer Jules Sandeau, and it is believed she initially took her pen name from him in return for his help. She was notorious for her affairs with Frédéric Chopin and Alfred de Musset. It is claimed that she based characters in her works on both of these men quite freely —after they had ended their relationships.

2. Robert Louis Stevenson was born in Scotland, a locale that shows up in *A Child's Garden of Verses,* a delightful book of poetry for children. Among his most famous books were *Treasure Island* and *Kidnapped.* He married an American, Fanny Osbourne, and despite his illness, traveled extensively. He spent his last years in Samoa, where he died, and was buried on a hillside looking out to sea, as he had requested in one of his poems. He was only forty-four when he died suddenly of an "apoplexy."

3. Nathaniel Hawthorne. Best known for his portrayal of New England Puritanism in *The Scarlet Letter,* he also wrote about his travels in England and Italy.

4. Colette. Her real name was Sidonie Gabrielle Claudine Colette. She was a young girl when she married her first husband, who set her to work writing. Not until she began writing under the name Colette did she become rich and famous. (Her husband had published her previous works under his name.) Her books about the schoolgirl "Claudine" became so famous that dresses, hair styles, and a whole school of fashion sprang up around this character. Colette was also noted for her romances, some of them scandalous even for that rather free era. She often said that she would die happy if she could reside in the Palais Royal, a particularly charming building and arcaded square in Paris. One of her admirers gave his Paris apartment to her for the rest of her life. (Since apartments in the Palais Royal have always been nearly impossible to obtain, this was a princely gesture.)

5. [William] Wilkie Collins (his first name is usually omitted). His best-known book is *The Woman in White,* which, along with *The Moonstone,* has assured his place in literature. Collins is generally credited with having established the genre, in English literature, of the mystery story.

6. Percy Bysshe Shelley. His second wife was Mary Wollstonecraft, the author of *Frankenstein.* Mary's mother, also Mary, was the author of *A Vindication of the Rights of Woman.* Mary's father was an advocate of "free love" and many other advanced ideas, but he was absolutely furious when his daughter, still in her teens, eloped with Shelley, who was married to someone else at the time. When Shelley's first wife committed suicide shortly thereafter, Shelley and Mary were married, but her father was not appeased.

7. James Michener. His specialty is to focus on a geographical area, and go back as far in time as he can, drawing a rich, full panorama with hundreds of characters and a long historical perspective. Among his books are *Centennial, The Source, Hawaii,* and *Poland.* A short story collection was named *Tales of the South Pacific.*

8. Anthony Trollope. His mother, Frances Trollope, found herself very much criticized in the United States after she wrote *Domestic Manners of the Americans,* a portrait of a rough, frontier society. Trollope also wrote about his travels in the United States, but he is probably best known for *Barchester Towers,* one in a series of novels called the Barsetshire Chronicles. His characters acquired new life when their descendants, often bearing the same names, were picked up by Angela Thirkell, long after his death, in her chronicles of Barsetshire. Her novels started prior to World War II, and continued through the period shortly after the end of the war.

9. Victor Hugo. Hugo was a man of immense vitality and convictions. He was an accomplished author as well as a painter, sketcher, satirist, and playwright. His most famous work, along with *The Hunchback of Notre Dame,* may well be *Les Misérables,* from which many characters, like Jean Valjean and Inspec-

tor Javert, have passed into a semifolkloric status. Hugo had to flee France during the restoration of the Second Empire and lived in Guernsey, where his house is now a museum. Although married, he also took his long-time mistress to Guernsey and provided her with a house that can be seen from the room he used as his bedroom, but not from the room Mrs. Hugo inhabited. This romance, incidentally, lasted most of his adult life. He was given one of the most enormous funerals France has ever seen. (He was also in politics as a senator.)

10. Raphael Sabatini. English-born Italian author. His best-known work is probably *Scaramouche,* a thrilling adventure tale that captivated readers of the 1920s. His literary career spanned about ten years, during which time he was intensely popular, and then ended, as far as the literary world was concerned.

II.

1. e. Voltaire, though in poor health and unable to do all he wanted, nonetheless managed to write and to influence the great men of his time. Voltaire spent a good deal of time in England, having sought refuge there because of the unpopularity of his ideas in France. When he returned to his homeland, he introduced Shakespeare to France, although eventually he came to dislike Shakespeare's works. After a stormy career, including several years at the court of Frederick the Great, he eventually came back to Paris a short time before his death. He was wined, dined, and feted, literally to death, although he was, after all, eighty-four when he died.

2. g. The gentleman with the aristocratic-sounding name seems to have written about forty million words about Nick Carter, detective. This was the original of the dime novels of detectives from the hard-boiled school. He also published the *Nick Carter Weekly,* allegedly written by Nick Carter himself. Some authorities also credit him with some romantic novels written under the pseudonym of Bertha N. Clay, which was the pseudonym of an Englishwoman named Charlotte E. Braeme, who died in 1884. But, since some books were written under that name after

Braeme's death, suspicion fell on the creator of Nick Carter. The whole affair requires the services of a good detective to unravel.

3. a. His simple tales, touching and heartwarming, about the life of a Yorkshire veterinarian, have sold in the millions. Such books as *All Things Bright and Beautiful* and *All Creatures Great and Small* relate the lives of the farmers of the Yorkshire dales and their animals in very human terms.

4. b. This wasn't exactly fair, as his middle name was Henri, which might have given more of a clue. Marie is often used for men as a given name in France, as is Anne.

5. d. This author wrote short stories—the most famous of which is probably *The Gift of the Magi*. His book of short stories, *The Four Million* (the then population of New York), concerns city life. His stories all have a "twist," which came to be the distinguishing feature of an O. Henry story. Few have portrayed working-class New York so interestingly.

6. c. The genius of the three Brontë sisters showed itself early. Charlotte's chief work was *Jane Eyre,* her sister Emily wrote *Wuthering Heights,* and another sister, Anne, wrote *The Tenant of Wildfell Hall.* All of the Brontës, including their brother, Branwell, died very young: none reached forty, and two died in their twenties. All succumbed to tuberculosis before they had a chance to show how much more they might have done.

7. h. This British novelist and critic is perhaps most famous for his novel, *A Clockwork Orange.* His works feature much wordplay and a rather grim view of life.

8. f. Eric Blair wrote *1984* as a warning of the way in which he saw the world going. While some feel that there are aspects of life today that he correctly warned of, it is also interesting to note that he originally planned to call the book *1948*. Blair also wrote a number of other books and essays about the seamy side of life in big cities and the evils of colonialism, but is better known for this and for *Animal Farm,* a satire.

9. j. Gardner was such a prolific writer that he could dictate a Perry

Mason detective novel in a few days. This incredibly prolific author used a variety of pen names to avoid appearing on the shelves in too great quantity, probably to avoid over-exposing Perry Mason.

10. i. These two functioned for many years as Ellery Queen. Ellery Queen was the hero of many of the novels allegedly written by himself, like Nick Carter. In his case, too, the creation of the authors achieved an independent existence, quite apart from the books, and many people believed he was real. (This happened to the character created by Georges Simenon, Inspector Maigret of the Paris police, as well as to Sherlock Holmes.)

III. *Just as a relief from facts:*

MARLOWE   STEVENSON   ROSSINI   KEATS   KIPLING

Rossini, an opera composer, is the odd man out.

IV. *This simple cryptogram was created by moving the alphabet down one letter so that A = B, and so on.*

"IT TOOK ME FIFTEEN YEARS TO DISCOVER THAT I HAD NO TALENT FOR WRITING, BUT I COULDN'T GIVE IT UP BECAUSE BY THAT TIME I WAS TOO FAMOUS." BENCHLEY.

V. *Any four of these will be correct:* "The Miller's Tale"; "The Reeve's Tale"; "The Man of Law's Tale"; "The Wife of Bath's Tale"; "The Clerk's Tale"; "The Squire's Tale"; "The Franklin's Tale"; "The Pardoner's Tale"; "The Prioress's Tale"; "The Manciple's Tale"; "The Summoner's Tale"; "The Monk's Tale"; "The Canon Yeoman's Tale"; "The Parson's Tale." *For explanation: a reeve was a high official; a franklin was a freeholder, ranking just below the gentry; a pardoner was licensed to sell papal pardons; a manciple bought provisions for an Inn of Court, or sometimes a monastery.*

Several other works by Chaucer were The Parliament of Fowls, Troilus and Criseyde, The Legend of Good Women, The Book of the Duchess, Anelida and Arcite, The House of Fame, *and* Boece *(a translation of Boethius's* The Consolation of Philosophy*).*

VI.

1. *The Grapes of Wrath*
2. *The Old Man and the Sea*
3. *A Fable (1955)* and *The Reivers (1963)*
4. *Gone With the Wind*
5. *Rabbit Is Rich*
6. *A Death in the Family*
7. *Collected Stories of Katherine Anne Porter*
8. *Humboldt's Gift*
9. *Advise and Consent*
10. *To Kill a Mockingbird*

Normally the recipient of a Pulitzer Prize is assured of comparatively lasting fame. There have been some exceptions, however. The award was given in 1934 to Caroline Miller for Lamb in His Bosom and, while she wrote other works, none ever achieved any degree of fame. The same can be said for Martin Flavin's Journey in the Dark, which received the award in 1944.

VII. *Start at the lower left-hand corner and you will find*
HOLMES, FROST, BENET, KEATS, POE, SHELLEY, MILLAY, WHITMAN.

VIII. *Pepys wrote his Diary in cipher. He fell out of favor in England because of his Stuart sympathies, and in all probability wrote in a cipher to protect himself. He left his diaries to his nephew, but it was not until the 1890s that they were completely deciphered and published in their present form.*

Boswell's papers, including much unpublished material, were found in an old closet and in a chest in Malahide Castle (near Dublin, Ireland), which is owned by one of his descendants. A Colonel Isham bought the papers and Yale University later purchased more, but this was not until fairly late in the twentieth century. Boswell died in 1795, and his papers had been unknowingly stored in the castle for almost two hundred years.

IX. *Samuel Taylor Coleridge dreamed "Kubla Khan." He said that he dreamed the poem after reading a description of Kublai Khan's palace, and that he began writing the poem as soon as he awakened. He was interrupted, according to the story, by a "person from Por-*

lock" *who wanted to see him, and when the visit was over, Coleridge had forgotten the rest. There is one theory that it was opium inspired.*
Robert Louis Stevenson stated that he dreamed the plot of Dr. Jekyll and Mr. Hyde.

X.

1. Ecclesiastes 19

2. This is FitzGerald's translation of the *Rubáiyát of Omar Khayyám*, stanza 13.

3. This has been attributed to Sophie Tucker in several reference books, without a specific date or time.

4. Ernest Hemingway, in *The Snows of Kilimanjaro*.

5. Anthony Trollope, *Dr. Thorne*, chapter 18.

6. Washington Irving, "The Creole Villages."

7. A. E. Housman, the poem "A Shropshire Lad." (As an offbeat side note, on a trip to China in 1983, this poem was quoted to the author by the Chinese guide, with a request for an explanation of several words.)

8. George Gordon, Lord Byron, *Childe Harold's Pilgrimage*, I, stanza 9.

9. George Bernard Shaw, *Maxims for Revolutionaries*.

10. Several authorities give this poem—or song—to W. J. Mondale in the 1850s. He seems to have been a music-hall performer. Other people have used the words and refrain on numerous occasions, usually attributing it to that well-known writer, Anon. The words are usually given as "Up and down the City Road, and in and out the Eagle. . . ." One explanation given is that the City Road was the location of a London pub frequented by hatters, who when they were out of money would pawn (or "pop") one of their more portable tools, a "weasel."

XI. *Each of the men named was convicted and either escaped or fled or actually served time in prison.*

1. O. Henry served time for embezzlement in Texas. Many researchers now believe that he was not guilty, and that sloppy bookkeeping practices at the bank where he worked led to the damaging shortage.

2. Richard Lovelace served time in prison for his Royalist sentiments. He was one of the Cavalier poets and was noted for his charm and wit. Probably his most famous poem, written while in confinement, contains the line "Stone walls do not a prison make/ Nor iron bars a cage."

3. Leigh Hunt served two years in prison for writing articles attacking King George IV of England. It is reported that he painted his cell with flowers and entertained lavishly (as was allowed upon payment to the jailers). His most famous poems are "Abou Ben Adhem" and "Jenny Kissed Me." (Incidentally, the Jenny referred to in his charming little rondeau was Jane Welsh Carlyle, wife of Thomas Carlyle.)

4. Victor Hugo's writings and politics got him into difficulties with the government on numerous occasions. He fled France several times to escape prison, going once to Guernsey in the Channel Islands and once to England. He refused to return to France until Napoleon II interceded.

5. John Bunyan, the nonconformist religious leader, served time in jail for his beliefs. His most famous work, the allegory *The Pilgrim's Progress from This World to That Which Is to Come,* commonly called *The Pilgrim's Progress,* is still widely read and was one of the most influential religious books of all time.

6. François Villon was the epitome of rascality and romance of the Late Middle Ages. He was well educated for his time, with both a Bachelor's and a Master's degree from the Sorbonne. He was arrested on various occasions for participating in robberies and murders and eventually sentenced to be hanged. However, possibly through the influence of powerful relatives, his sentence was commuted to ten years' banishment from Paris. He left Paris and disappeared from history's pages.

7. Oscar Wilde, a leader of the Aesthetic movement, wit, poet, playwright, and homosexual, made one of the major mistakes of

literary history when he sued the Marquess of Queensberry for libel—and lost. The evidence brought out at the trial led to a charge of "indecent acts," for which Wilde spent two years in prison, at Reading Gaol, where he wrote his famous, heartrending poem, *The Ballad of Reading Gaol*. It is literally a cry from his soul, as he states. On his release in 1897, he fled to Paris, where he lived for a few years, before dying in 1900 at forty-six. His last words are alleged to have been, "I am dying beyond my means."

8. Sir Thomas More, statesman and writer, though a good friend of King Henry VIII, would not swear allegiance to the King as head of the Church of England. Henry, with his customary unforgiving temperament, had More beheaded.

9. André (Marie de) Chénier, poet, was initially sympathetic to the French Revolution and was associated with its leader, Robespierre. Chénier was later sickened by the excesses committed in the name of the revolution and expressed his disillusionment to Robespierre. He was executed in 1794, only a few days before the end of the Reign of Terror.

10. This naturalistic writer was perhaps most famous for his letter in defense of Captain Alfred Dreyfus, *J'accuse* (I accuse), which earned him the hatred of the extremely anti-Dreyfus government. Zola was prosecuted for libel and fled to England to avoid imprisonment. He died of carbon monoxide poisoning in Paris in 1902.

XII.

1. c. Shangri-La was the invention of James Hilton. The imaginary world, hidden high in the Himalayas, was a paradise where one never grew old. The book was made into a highly successful movie.

2. e. Sir Thomas More wrote this classic, whose name has become a synonym for a perfect place or an earthly paradise. It was originally written in Latin.

3. a. Erewhon, "nowhere" spelled backward (almost), is the creation of Samuel Butler.

4. j. Gopher Prairie was the invention of Sinclair Lewis, the archetype of a small town in the American Midwest, defined by its prejudices, mores, and narrowmindedness.

5. f. This cathedral town, invented by Anthony Trollope, was modeled on a real town in southern England.

6. d. Lilliput is one of the countries visited by Gulliver in the famous *Gulliver's Travels* by Jonathan Swift. Although often seen as a book for children, *Gulliver's Travels* was actually a biting political satire of its time.

7. i. La Mancha is the land traveled by Don Quixote, the character created by Cervantes.

8. h. Brigadoon is a mythical Scottish town that appears for one day every hundred years. The musical comedy about this enchanted town was written by Alan Jay Lerner (book and lyrics) and Frederick Loewe (music).

9. g. Ruritania is a mythical kingdom, the home of Prince Rupert of Hentzau. The novel, *The Prisoner of Zenda,* and its sequel, *Rupert of Hentzau,* were written by Anthony Hope Hawkins. The novels, and the plays made from them, were highly successful commercially. Ronald Colman starred in the movie, made after the success of the two stage adaptations.

10. b. Serendip was the ancient name for Ceylon, but that is not the source of the current word. That came from the novel by Horace Walpole about the three princes of Serendip who were always making happy discoveries by accident. Thus the noun *serendipity* was coined.

XIII.

1. e. Roosevelt wrote, among many other books, *Winning of the West.* He was the prolific author of several commercially successful books.

2. g. Jefferson was the chief author of the Declaration of Independence. Many others, including Benjamin Franklin, worked on this document.

3. f. Wilson's *A History of the American People* appeared in five volumes. This scholarly author was once president of Princeton University.

4. b. Nixon has written many other works on political theories, and his memoirs.

5. j. Adams's writings were not published in a definitive edition until after his death.

6. d. *At Ease.* Eisenhower wrote many other books, but this one best reveals him as an individual.

7. h. Grant, penniless and dying of throat cancer, wrote his autobiography in the hope that earnings from it would provide for his family. *Personal Memoirs* earned them close to $500,000.

8. i. Kennedy accepted the Pulitzer Prize for this book.

9. c. Hoover was a renowned mining engineer.

10. d. Madison was assisted by Alexander Hamilton and John Jay in writing *The Federalist Papers,* an eloquent defense of the Constitution, which Madison played a large part in shaping.

CHAPTER 2

Quotes with Notes

Capping someone's quote is a favorite sport for many. There is no joy like that of a confirmed quotation addict who hears a friend misquote, even slightly, a well-known remark. It is a great source of pride to be able to correct even the smallest of errors.

The following quizzes include correct and incorrect quotations, identification of authors of famous quotations, some questions about the individuals to whom the quotations refer, and similar mind-stretching mental exercises guaranteed to make the quotation enthusiast pick up at least a few more morsels.

I.
In this question, designed to test your memory for quotations, one word or one phrase has been omitted. Fill in the missing word or phrase.

1. Wine is a mocker, ___ ___ ___ ___ (4 words)

2. The harp that once ___ ___ ___ (3 words) The soul of music shed. . . .

3. They dined on ___ , and slices of ___
   Which they ate with a ___ (1 word) spoon
   And hand in hand, on the edge of the sand,
   They danced by the light of the moon.

4. For he who lives more lives than one,
   ___ ___ ___ ___ ___ ___ (6 words)

5. Breathes there a man with soul so dead
   Who never to himself hath said,
   ____ ____ ____ ____ ____ ____ ____ (7 words, plus comma and
   exclamation point)

6. Alas, poor Yorick ____ ____ ____ ____ (4 words)

7. The Assyrian came down like the wolf on the fold,
   And ____ ____ ____ ____ ____ ____ ____ ____ (8 words)

8. A bit of talcum
   ____ ____ ____ (3 words—and they must be spelled as in the
   original)

9. I have nothing to offer but blood ____, ____ ____ ____ (4 words)

10. Don't look back. ____ ____ ____ ____ ____ ____ (6 words)

II.

*This section contains quotations on the topic of Love. Match the
following quotation with its author.*

1. Ah, love, let us be true
   To one another! For the world, which seems
   To lie before us like a land of dreams,
   So various, so beautiful, so new,
   Hath really neither joy, nor love, nor light,
   Nor certitude, nor peace, nor help for pain;
   And we are here as on a darkling plain
   Swept with confused alarms of struggle and flight,
   Where ignorant armies clash by night.

2. Men have died from time to time,
   and worms have eaten them, but not for love.

3. What is love? tis not hereafter:
   Present mirth hath present laughter.
   What's to come is still unsure
   In delay there lies no plenty,
   Then come and kiss me, sweet and twenty,
   Youth's a stuff will not endure.

4. In the spring a young man's fancy
   lightly turns to thoughts of love, . . .

5. You say to me-wards your affection's strong;
   Pray love me little, so you love me long.

6. True love is like ghosts, which everybody talks about and few
   have seen.

7. That Love is all there is
   Is all we know of Love,
   It is enough, the freight should be
   Proportioned to the groove.

8. The only difference between a caprice and a lifelong passion is
   that the caprice lasts a little longer.

9. Love is not all; it is not meat nor drink
   Nor slumber nor a roof against the rain;
   Nor yet a floating spar to men that sink.

10. The fairest things have fleetest end.
    Their scent survives their close;
    But the rose's scent is bitterness
    To him that loved the rose.

a. William Shakespeare, from *Twelfth Night*

b. Alfred, Lord Tennyson, "Locksley Hall"

c. William Shakespeare, from *As You Like It*

d. Matthew Arnold, "Dover Beach"

e. Francis Thompson, "Daisy"

f. Edna St. Vincent Millay "Love is not All"

g. François, Duc de la Rochefoucald, *Sentences and Moral Maxims*

h. Robert Herrick, "Love Me Little, Love Me Long"

i. Emily Dickinson, No. 1765

j. Oscar Wilde, from *The Picture of Dorian Gray*

III.

In this particular literary teaser, you are expected to name the person about whom the quotation was written or spoken. They are not particularly obvious, but all are reasonably famous individuals.

1. [He] has a lean and hungry look: He thinks too much: such men are dangerous. _____

2. Thy beauty is to me,/Like those Nicean barques of yore,/That gently, o'er a perfumed sea,/The weary, wayworn wanderer bore/To his own native shore. _____

3. He nothing common did or mean
   Upon that memorable scene . . . _____

4. I have found it impossible to carry the heavy burden of responsibility . . . without the help and support of the woman I love. (Who was she?) _____

5. He don't plant 'taters, he don't plant cotton;/And them that plants them, is soon forgotten . . . _____

6. I beheld the wretch, the miserable being whom I had created. _____

7. To the memory of the Man, first in war, first in peace, and first in the hearts of his countrymen. _____

8. I used to say of him, that his presence on the field made the difference of forty thousand men. _____

9. Oh, but he was a tightfisted hand at the grindstone . . . squeezing, wrenching, grasping, scraping, clutching, covetous old sinner! . . . solitary as an oyster. _____

10. She is coming, my own, my sweet:
    Were it ever so airy a tread,
    My heart would hear her and beat,
    Were it earth in an earthy bed,
    My dust would hear her and beat,
    Had I lain for a century dead,
    Would start and tremble under her feet,
    And blossom in purple and red. _____

IV.

Parodies are always popular. Here are some famous, or infamous, parodies. Identify the original from which they were taken, and the parodist.

1. "You are old, Father William," the young man said,
   "And your hair has become very white,
   And yet you incessantly stand on your head,
   Do you think at your age it is right?"   _____

2. I think that I shall never see,
   A billboard lovely as a tree,
   In fact unless the billboards fall,
   I'll never see a tree at all.   _____

3. Still worse are these we daily see,
   It is but hadn't ought to be!   _____

4. Twinkle, twinkle little bat
   How I wonder what you're at
   Up above the world you fly
   Like a teatray in the sky.   _____

5. How doth the little crocodile
   Improve his shining tail,
   And pour the waters of the Nile
   On every golden scale.   _____

V.

Each of the following quotations, disparate though they may seem, is attributed to the same source. Identify the source.

1. The halls of fame are open wide
   And they are always full,
   Some go in by the door called "push,"
   And some by the door called "pull."

2. It's gude to be merry and wise
   It's gude to be honest and true
   Tis gude to be off the old love,
   Before you are on with the new.

3. Climb high
   Climb far
   Your goal the sky
   Your aim the star.

4. It's the same the whole world over,
   It's the poor wot gets the blame.
   It's the rich wot gets the pleasure,
   Ain't it all a bloomin' shame?

5. Education is what you have left over after you have
   forgotten everything you have learned.

VI.

You are given here the first lines of various poems whose last lines follow. Match up the beginnings and the endings.

1. Tell me not, sweet, I am unkind

2. I wandered lonely as a cloud

3. Thou still unravished bride of quietness

4. The year's at the spring,

5. Strew on her roses, roses,

6. A Garden is a lovesome thing, God wot!

7. Blow, blow, thou winter wind.

8. Gather ye rosebuds while ye may

9. Once upon a midnight dreary while I pondered,
   weak and weary

10. Out of the night that covers me, black as the pit
    from pole to pole

a. Beauty is truth, truth beauty,—that is all
   Ye know on earth, and all ye need to know.

b. All's right with the world.

c. 'Tis very sure God walks in mine.

d. The Vasty hall of death.

e. I am the master of my fate, I am the captain of my
  soul.

f. I could not love thee, dear, so much,
    Loved I not Honour more.

g. And dances with the daffodils.

h. This life is most jolly.

i. You may forever tarry.

j. And my soul from out that shadow that lies floating
  on the floor, shall be lifted, nevermore.

ANSWERS

I.

1. *Strong drink is raging.* Proverbs, 20:1 The Bible has a good many admonitions against strong drink—this is one of the shortest. See Proverbs 23:31–32 for additional admonitions against drinking.

2. The harp that once *through Tara's halls*/The soul of music shed/ Now hangs as mute on Tara's walls/As if that soul were fled. From the Irish song "The Harp that Once Through Tara's Halls." The author was George Moore. Tara was originally, of course, the great hall in Meath, Ireland, called the Hill of Tara. It was a meeting place for the Irish kings, clergy, bards, and princes to discuss and consult on public affairs.

3. *Quince, mince, runcible.* This, of course, is the *Owl and the Pussycat* by Edward Lear. The nonsense word *runcible,* for no reason that I have been able to determine, has been applied to a broad three-tined pickle fork. It might equally well have been applied to an oyster fork, an olive fork, or anything else, but someone along the line decided to call this particular fork a run-cible spoon. I can only report, not explain.

4. *More lives than one must die.* This is from *The Ballad of Reading Gaol,* which was written by Oscar Wilde while he was serving a prison term as the result of his ill-conceived suit for slander, which backfired.

5. *This is my own, my native land!* From "The Lay of the Last Minstrel," by Sir Walter Scott. It is also the poem that Philip Nolan was reading in the short story *The Man Without a Country* when he choked and threw the book away.

6. Alas, poor Yorick, *I knew him, Horatio.* Shakespeare, naturally, Hamlet, V, i, 201. It is *not,* as often misquoted, "Alas, poor Yorick, I knew him well." This is one of the misquotes most often misquoted.

7. *his cohorts were gleaming in purple and gold*
And the sheen of their spears was like stars on the sea,
When the blue wave rolls nightly on deep Galilee.

From *The Destruction of Sennacherib,* by George Gordon, Lord Byron.

8. A bit of talcum
    Is always walcum.
    None other than Ogden Nash, naturally, with that flawed but flawless rhyme at the end.

9. *toil, sweat and tears.* This quotation from Winston Churchill is usually misquoted, without the word *toil,* as "blood, sweat and tears." The original recording of his speech can be heard in London, in the War Rooms, a restoration of British headquarters during the Battle of Britain.

10. *Something may be gaining on you.* The quotation is from the immortal and unforgettable Leroy ("Satchel") Paige's *How to Keep Young.*

II.

1. d.	6. g.
2. c.	7. i.
3. a.	8. j.
4. b.	9. f.
5. h.	10. e.

III.

1. The description is of Cassius, in Shakespeare's *Julius Caesar.* Not under quite the same circumstances, nor for the same reasons, it has been said that you cannot trust thin cooks.

2. Helen was the lady whose beauty was praised in the poem of the same name by Edgar Allan Poe.

3. The description is of King Charles I at his own execution, and was written by poet Andrew Marvell several years later.

4. The famous abdication speech of King Edward VIII (so-called, although he was never officially crowned), in which he renounced his throne in order to marry the American Wallis Warfield Simpson, who had been divorced and was thus doubly ineligible to marry the king.

5. The "he" is Ole Man River in the song written by Oscar Hammerstein and Jerome Kern for the musical comedy *Showboat*.

6. Mary Wollstonecraft Shelley, wife of Percy Bysshe Shelley, wrote this description of Frankenstein's monster in the book *Frankenstein*.

7. This is the famous description of George Washington delivered in a resolution presented to the House of Representatives by Light-horse Harry Lee on the occasion of Washington's death.

8. The Duke of Wellington described Napoleon Bonaparte in these terms.

9. Charles Dickens is the author of this description of Ebenezer Scrooge in his *A Christmas Carol*.

10. This bit of purple poetry and romantic effusion is by Alfred, Lord Tennyson, and can be found, if you wish to look for it, in "Maud," part 1, stanza 11. (It was set to music by Balfe, and sung by the great tenor John McCormack.)

IV.

1. The parody is by Lewis Carroll. The original, "The Old Man's Comforts and How He Gained Them," is by Robert Southey and runs:

> "You are old, Father William," the young man cried,
> "The few locks which are left you are gray,
> You are hale, Father William—a hearty old man
> Now tell me the reason, I pray."

2. Parody by Ogden Nash. Original by Joyce Kilmer, his famous poem "Trees."

> I think that I shall never see,
> A poem lovely as a tree . . .

3. This is from Bret Harte's parody on John Greenleaf Whittier's poem "Maud Muller." The original poem is about the judge who saw the lovely Maud Muller on a farm but did not marry her because she was only a poor farmer's daughter. He later regretted it, according to Whittier's poem, which ends "For of all sad words

of tongue or pen/The saddest are these, It might have been." The spoof by Harte includes the quoted words, and also discusses what happened when the judge *did* marry lovely, innocent, uneducated Maud Muller. As Harte wrote, "For there be women fair as she/ Whose verbs and nouns do more agree." The poem is "Mrs. Judge Jenkins."

4. The original is the nursery rhyme, "Twinkle, twinkle little star." Again, a parody by Lewis Carroll.

5. Parody by Lewis Carroll. Isaac Watts, who wrote a great deal of moralistic verse, produced the original, called "Divine Song, XX."

> How doth the little busy bee
> Improve each shining hour
> And gather honey all the day
> From every opening flower.

Watts was also chosen by Carroll for another parody, the one that begins "Tis the voice of the lobster, I heard him declare, you have baked me too brown, I must sugar my hair." This is a take-off on Watts's poem

> Tis the voice of the sluggard,
> I heard him complain
> You have waked me too early
> I must slumber again.

V. *All of the quotations are indeed from one source, that well-known character Anon. They are folksongs, quotations, and a potpourri of well-known expressions. You may find Stanley Baldwin listed as the author of the Push-Pull quatrain, but he specifically stated when he said these lines that he was quoting.*

There is also another variant of the quatrain in number 2, which ends,

> *Tis well to be on with the new love.*
> *Before you are off with the old.*

Take your pick.

VI.

1. f. This is from "To Lucasta, Going to the Wars," by Richard Lovelace, the Cavalier poet who died young and in poverty. Prob-

CHAPTER 3

The Name Is Familiar

There are many characters from fiction whose names live on as synonyms for a particular type of personality. Mrs. Malaprop, for example, discussing an "allegory on the banks of the Nile," has passed into the literature and that title is now applied to an amusing misuse of a word. The Midas touch, from the folk tale, describes a touch that turns everything to gold. The tale ended unhappily for King Midas, but there is no sense of opprobrium when someone is described as having this gift of turning everything to gold; it usually implies extreme wealth or luck. Uriah Heep has passed into the popular imagination as an unctuous villain who cloaks his villainy with the claim, "I'm 'umble." Other characters are immediately recognizable to the literary mind.

I.

Since you, dear reader, have a literary mind (you would not have gotten this far if you had not), a list of ten female characters follows. Also following is a description of each character. Names and characters are scrambled, of course. Match the women on the left with the characteristics attributed to them on the right, and see how well you know your heroines (or villainesses as the case may be). The first list is, as stated, of women. It would be too easy if men were included, but so as not to be unfair, a similar list of men follows, as Question II.

1. Emma Bovary
2. Elaine the Lily Maid
3. Madame Defarge
4. Anna Karenina
5. Portia

6. Pollyanna
7. Marguerite Gauthier
8. Mrs. Grundy
9. Hester Prynne
10. Anna Livia Plurabelle

a. The mother of an illegitimate child, she shields her lover until he gains the inner strength to confess.

b. This young lady has become symbolic of the kind of soppy sentimentalist who can see no problems, ever.

c. This is the name given to the heroine of a book by Alexandre Dumas the younger. In American adaptations and the translation of the play, she was called Camille, and in Verdi's opera *La Traviata,* she is Violetta.

d. The name used for a censorious and disapproving older woman who stands guard over the mores and manners of her neighbors.

e. The lady is the spirit of the river running through Dublin in a classic and much-discussed novel.

f. The wife of a country doctor, she searches for love in all the wrong places and finally kills herself, not for love, but for debts.

g. This aristocratic lady, married to an unfeeling husband, loves and is loved by someone closer to her spirit. Unable to live happily with her lover, she commits suicide.

h. This beautiful maiden loved Lancelot, but died under unusual circumstances; her body floated downriver to King Arthur's court.

i. She knitted while France murdered its elite.

j. This lady's name has come to be used for a female lawyer, as indicated by its use in this sense in a long-running radio soap opera.

II.

These are male characters who have come to symbolize types. Match the characters and their description.

1. Mr. Micawber
2. George F. Babbitt
3. Simon Legree
4. Scrooge
5. Lothario
6. Don Juan
7. Hiawatha
8. Dr. Jekyll and Mr. Hyde
9. Jeeves
10. Benedick

a. The quintessential American businessman, his name has passed into the language as a synonym for a commercially oriented crass individual.

b. The prototype of the noble savage.

c. Because of his conduct toward slaves in the book in which he appeared, this character is often used to describe a cruel and heartless taskmaster or boss.

d. A novella by Robert Louis Stevenson describes a kind man who changes himself into an evil one, showing that there are two sides to human nature.

e. The perennial optimist, who always looks for something to turn up.

f. The name has passed into the language as the synonym for the perfect butler, as immortalized by P. G. Wodehouse.

g. This wicked character was a mean and grasping miser who suffered a change of heart.

h. This character is the epitome of the sworn bachelor who ends up married.

i. This fellow has become the symbol of the heartless aristocratic libertine.

j. A young seducer of women.

III.

Each of the following people is associated with a particular kind of animal. The names of the individuals are on the left, the animals are on the right. Match person and animal—sometimes a pet, sometimes not.

1.	Elizabeth Barrett Browning	a.	Bucephalus
2.	Alexander the Great	b.	Beth Gelert
3.	Bellerophon	c.	Rocinante
4.	Lord Llewellyn, in W. R. Spencer's ballad	d.	Grani
5.	Don Quixote	e.	the peacock
6.	Captain Hook	f.	a spider
7.	Siegfried	g.	a ticking crocodile
8.	Mohammed	h.	Flush
9.	Robert Bruce	i.	Pegasus
10.	Juno	j.	Fadda

IV.

The following cryptogram, just for fun, is a quotation from one of the people listed in the test above. It is one of the best-known quotations from this real person, and has been parodied, rewritten, and variously abused. It was set to music, not too well, by Maude Valerie-White (a useful bit of trivia for you).

DMW EM F IMUA SDAA IAS JA VMTKS SDA WLYR

V.

1. The following quotation has had all the vowels removed and has then been broken up into groups of letters. Replace the vowels, find the correct word divisions, and reconstruct the quote. (There is one null letter.)

GLD NLD SND GRL SLL MST SCH MNY SWP RSC
MTD STx

2. *The following square has a short poem coiled within it. Start at the proper letter, move in any direction, and find the poem. (One null letter.)*

S	I	D	R	L	I	E	H	T	A
D	D	W	O	O	V	T	A	D	Y
E	A	H	W	T	S	N	I	G	Y
N	E	I	D	A	I	S	A	E	B
I	I	A	S	M	Y	Y	I	S	T
T	S	S	O	E	S	A	T	J	U

3. Each of the following names has been scrambled. First and last names have been given. What do all of the names have in common.

E L E O I O R G E G T   R N G D E S O A G E

N A O C B E L T L

ANSWERS

I.

1. f. Emma Bovary was Madame Bovary, in Flaubert's novel of the same name, the wife of Charles Bovary, a country doctor. Emma had hopelessly romantic ideas about herself as the heroine of a great love affair. Since her husband was far too prosaic a character for her, she sought romance outside her marriage, and accumulated vast debts to pay for fulfilling her illusions. Finally, seeing no way out of her plight, she committed suicide. This is one of the first great realistic novels of the nineteenth century, and a model for realistic novels that followed.

2. h. The lady in question, based loosely upon a figure in the Arthurian legend, is the heroine of Tennyson's poem, "Lancelot and Elaine," included in *Idylls of the King*. Elaine was condemned to see the world only in a mirror, but she was so struck by Lancelot that she looked out, died, and was sent down the river to the King's palace with a lily in her hand. The king had her buried with all the pomp and ceremony due a queen, which should have appeased Lancelot's conscience but didn't help.

3. i. Madame Defarge was the wife of a revolutionary during the French Revolution and enjoyed executions thoroughly. She sat at the foot of the guillotine, knitting incessantly, as the aristocrats were beheaded. (She must have had a strong stomach—accounts of the times relate that the odor was so horrible that householders for blocks around petitioned to have the guillotine moved from where it was to anyplace else.) She existed only in Charles Dickens's book *A Tale of Two Cities*.

4. g. Literature of the nineteenth century is full of such stories, realistic, powerful, and examining the desire of women for more than they had, especially in the romantic area. Anna Karenina, like Madame Bovary, although of a much higher social class, suffers the same vicissitudes of love. She, however, loves and is loved in return. But in the Russia of those days divorce was impossible, and so she abandoned her husband and shamed him, herself, and her lover, and became permanently estranged from her children.

5. j. The brilliant closely reasoning young woman in *The Merchant of Venice* by Shakespeare. By a clever piece of analysis, she helps the eponymous merchant avoid paying a pound of flesh as payment for a debt. She is also a rich heiress. Among those who speak in clichés, the name is a synonym for female lawyers.

6. b. Pollyanna, the Glad Girl, was an enormous success in a book by the same name by Eleanor H. Porter. This angelic and optimistic child saw the best in everyone, the good in everything, and always played "The Glad Game," telling herself and others to be glad about various misfortunes and problems. The book does not record how many people tried to kill her for her eternal cheerfulness.

7. c. The name given by Alexandre Dumas the younger to the heroine of his play. In the American versions, the heroine was called Camille, apparently because the play was titled *The Lady of the Camelias*. As indicated earlier, Verdi called her Violetta Valery in *La Traviata*. The character of this Parisian courtesan, who gives up the man she loves to save him from ruin, was based on the real-life Madeleine du Plessis, who died in her early twenties of tuberculosis.

8. d. The identity of the original Mrs. Grundy is the subject of some dispute, but the phrase "What will Mrs. Grundy say?" was widely used to indicate disapproval and criticism of an action. There are several candidates for the role, but apparently the first recorded instance was in the play "Speed the Plow," which was written by Tom Morton and first produced in 1798. There are many later allusions to Mrs. Grundy, but the story that the name came from the wife of a Tennessee legislator who lived in Washington is a little hard to credit, as the first use of the name predates his legislative service.

9. a. Hester Prynne is the heroine of *The Scarlet Letter*. When her child was born in the absence of her husband, she was pilloried but refused to name the man responsible. Her husband returned, suspected the young minister, accurately, and hounded the minister, Dimsdale, until he confessed publicly. Thus unburdened, he died. It is one of Hawthorne's gloomy, realistic, brooding New England novels of Puritanism.

10. e. This character is from James Joyce's *Finnegans Wake,* and represents all women and is the personification of the River Liffey, which flows through Dublin, where the novel is set.

II.

1. e. Mr. Micawber was always looking for something to turn up. He lived in a state of perpetual hope that some stroke of good fortune would arrive in time to save him from debt.

2. a. Sinclair Lewis wrote about Babbitt, his business affairs, and life in America in the twenties. If undated, and updated only slightly with just topical references, it could probably pass as a current novel. Babbitt does try to break away, but he misses his chains and returns to his business, his family, and his sense of order and security. He is, however, a more sympathetic figure than his name has come to signify.

3. c. A "regular Simon Legree" is still a fitting epitaph for a cruel and unfeeling boss, and is taken from Harriet Beecher Stowe's portrait of a plantation owner in *Uncle Tom's Cabin.*

4. g. The immortal character of Scrooge, with his "Bah, Humbug!" and his miserly ways, has also passed into the English language. Scrooge suffered, or enjoyed, depending on your viewpoint, a complete change of heart in *A Christmas Carol* and became a generous and loving human being.

5. j. A Lothario, not quite as pejorative as a Don Juan, is something of a ladies' man, or even a gigolo. He originally appeared in Nicholas Rowe's tragedy *The Fair Penitent* in 1703.

6. i. Don Juan has come to stand for the dedicated libertine, the professional seducer. One of the first authors to relate his legend was Gabriel Tellez in the seventeenth century. Later authors include Molière, Byron, Shaw, Merimée, Dumas the elder, Musset, Balzac, Flaubert, and Pushkin. Mozart contributed an operatic version of this tale, *Don Giovanni.*

7. b. The noble savage was extolled in stories like Fenimore Cooper's five-volume *Leatherstocking Tales* and Longfellow's poem *Hiawatha.* While many books and movies have been based on

the philosophy that "the only good Indian is a dead Indian," Hiawatha, an Ojibway Indian, not surprisingly preached peace with the white man.

8. d. Robert Louis Stevenson wrote *The Strange Case of Dr. Jekyll and Mr. Hyde* in 1886. The doctor is a good man who turns himself into Mr. Hyde, an evil character, with a potion and takes another potion to turn himself back. Eventually, the evil Hyde becomes stronger and commits a murder. The doctor, to his horror, finds he cannot change back into his real self. He commits suicide.

9. f. Jeeves is the perfect butler and serves Bertie Wooster, a member of the Drones Club, in many novels by P. G. Wodehouse. Jeeves is smart, resourceful, and intelligent enough to keep Bertie from realizing that he's smarter than his employer. Jeeves is now a synonym for the perfect manservant.

10. h. The chief awareness of this term for a single man is from *Much Ado About Nothing* by Shakespeare. The name was probably taken from St. Benedict, who, sworn to celibacy, was vehement in his defense of that state.

III.

1. h. Flush was Elizabeth Barrett Browning's little dog. It played a large part in the stage production of *The Barretts of Wimpole Street*. Elizabeth Barrett was a devoted dog owner and took Flush with her when she eloped with Robert Browning. The dog even accompanied her to the church where they were married. Afterward, Elizabeth returned to her family home, while Browning arranged an elopement to Italy for them. And, nice to relate, they lived happily ever after.

2. a. Bucephalus was the famous horse of Alexander the Great. His name comes from the Greek *boukephalos*, or bull-headed. This was not meant to refer to his character, but to his appearance. There was an oracle which stated that the tamer of this horse would be the ruler of Macedonia. Alexander tamed Bucephalus and won the throne. Bucephalus was not Alexander's only horse, but he was his favorite.

3. i. Pegasus is the name of two different horses in Greek lore, according to some sources. Originally it was the horse of the Muses, born of sea foam, and the blood of the murdered Medusa. In another story, Bellerophon, killer of the Chimaera, tried to ride to Heaven on Pegasus, but was thrown. Pegasus was also used by Apollo and figures in the story of Perseus and Andromeda.

4. b. In this W. R. Spencer ballad, Beth Gelert was the faithful dog who saved Lord Llewellyn's child from a wolf and was killed by Llewellyn, who drew the wrong conclusion when he found the child's cradle empty and bloodied and Beth Gelert covered with blood.

5. c. Rocinante was the faithful horse, all skin and bones, ridden by the Don on his quixotic adventures. Did you remember that Sancho Panza rode an ass named Dapple?

6. g. The sworn enemy of Peter Pan, Captain Hook, had lost a portion of himself to a crocodile. The crocodile apparently liked the flavor of the captain so much that it followed him around ceaselessly, hoping to grab another choice morsel. Fortunately for all concerned, except the crocodile, it had also swallowed a ticking clock, which gave warning of its approach. On one occasion, Peter Pan saved himself by imitating the ticking of the clock.

7. d. Siegfried's horse, in Wagner's works.

8. j. Fadda was Mohammed's mule.

9. f. Robert Bruce was a chieftain who became King of Scotland in 1306. He is a prominent character in the book *Scottish Chiefs* by Jane Porter. Bruce had been crowned king but had been defeated in battles subsequently. Hiding in a cave one day, he noticed a spider trying to spin a web. It tried six times and failed, but succeeded on the seventh try. Bruce said that he too had failed six times, but would try once more. He did so, and conquered most of Scotland, which he reclaimed from the English. In 1328 Edward III recognized Scotland's independence, which lasted until Queen Elizabeth I's successor became king of both England and Scotland, so that the two countries were united under one ruler, as they are now.

10. e. In Roman mythology, Juno, the wife of Jupiter, was symbolized by the peacock. The play *Juno and the Paycock* by Sean O'Casey takes its title from this legend.

IV. *This is a cryptogram in which the word* love *has been used to encode the alphabet like this:*

L O V E A B C D F G H I J K M N P Q R S T U W X Y Z
A B C D E F G H I J K L M N O P Q R S T U V W X Y Z

HOW DO I LOVE THEE? LET ME COUNT THE WAYS.

V.

1. GOLDEN LADS AND GIRLS ALL MUST AS CHIMNEY SWEEPERS COME TO DUST

2. A Word is dead/When it is said,/Some say/I say it just/Begins to live,/That day. (Start at the A, near the center, fifth row from left.)

3. GEORGE ELIOT, GEORGE SAND, ACTON BELL. All were women writing under male pen names, Mary Ann Evans, Amandine Lucie Aurore Dupin, and Anne Brontë, respectively.

CHAPTER 4

Whodunit and Who Wrote It

As all aficionados know, one of the pleasures of reading detective stories or mysteries (the two are not necessarily synonymous) is following a favorite character, the brilliant or bumbling—as the case may be—detective, through his or her adventures. This also applies to those delightful series in which the minor characters are fully fleshed out. It is gratifying to follow the fortunes of a character you have come to like, even if that character is not the central figure. Many characters from detective and mystery stories have become real to their readers. Sherlock Holmes is so firmly perceived as a real person that many a tourist has looked in vain for 221B Baker Street. To cater to this demand, a London pub has set up a model of the room at 221B Baker Street, furnished just as described in the Conan Doyle stories, upstairs at the Sherlock Holmes Pub on Northumberland Street. Of course, people who go looking for Holmes's digs are probably the same people who send wedding gifts to soap opera characters when those characters get married, but the fact remains that many fictional characters have acquired independent lives.

Several sleuths have been turned into movie stars or stage characters with considerable success. Hard-boiled Sam Spade is one such example; Miss Marple, the gently witty, observant, knitting spinster is another. Lord Peter Wimsey, known to family and friends as Peter Death (pronounced *Deeth*) Bredon Wimsey, is yet another.

I.

For those who read detective stories regularly, these questions should be no real challenge. Even for those who don't, most have graduated from "detective fiction" to "literature," and these characters are generally well known.

Following is a list of famous detectives. On the right is a list of authors. Match characters with authors. (Some authors may appear more than once.)

1. Perry Mason	a.	J. J. Marric
2. Philip Marlowe	b.	John Creasey
3. Miss Jane Marple	c.	Erle Stanley Gardner
4. Hercule Poirot	d.	Agatha Christie
5. Inspector Maigret	e.	Margery Allingham
6. Nero Wolfe and Archie Goodwin	f.	Dorothy Sayers
7. Steve Carella	g.	Georges Simenon
8. Dr. Gideon Fell	h.	John Dickson Carr
9. Albert Campion	i.	Raymond Chandler
10. Inspector Roger West	j.	G. K. Chesterton
11. Commander George Gideon	k.	Bill Knox
12. Father Brown	l.	Leslie Charteris
13. The Saint	m.	Evan Hunter
14. Peter Wimsey	n.	Ngaio Marsh
15. Webb Carrick	o.	Rex Stout
16. Roderick Alleyn		

II.

The Sherlock Holmes Casebook: These are questions to test your memory. Holmes's prodigious memory was a large part of his success.

1. What was the name of Sherlock's brother?

2. Where did Holmes live before he moved to 221B Baker Street?

3. Holmes claimed a real person on his family tree. He stated that his grandmother was a relative of whom?

4. Watson had been wounded by a Jezail bullet in Afghanistan. What part of his anatomy had been hit?

5. Who was "The Woman"—as she is almost always referred to—in the stories?

6. What was "The Speckled Band" that figured so prominently in the story of that name?

7. Which Holmes adventure was initially begun in Utah and concerned the Church of the Latter-Day Saints?

8. Which Holmes adventure, far antedating LSD or other hallucinogenic drugs, depends for its solution on the ingestion of a strong hallucinogen?

9. What was the first name of Dr. Watson's wife?

10. Sir Arthur Conan Doyle stated that he modeled Holmes on a real person. Who was he? (Several candidates have been suggested, but this is the person whom Conan Doyle stated was his original inspiration.)

11. Where did Holmes's famous deerstalker hat and cloak originate?

ANSWERS

I.

1. c. This famous defense lawyer is the creation of Erle Stanley Gardner (who was also A. A. Fair). Perry Mason, with his charming sidekick Della Street, swashbuckled, dazzled, and bluffed his way through dozens of books and a television series. He was noted for his displays of legal erudition, his courtroom surprises, his unorthodox procedures, which made many lawyers wince, and his theatrical manner.

2. i. This prototype of the hard-boiled detective and forerunner of the tough-guy novel, Philip Marlowe was developed by Raymond Chandler. Chandler's writing seems so quintessentially American that it is surprising to learn he was brought up and educated in England, and did not return to the United States until he was nearly an adult. One of his most famous books, *The Lady in the Lake,* was translated into a movie with outstanding success. Others feel that *The Long Goodbye* and *The Big Sleep* are even better examples of his work.

3. d. Miss Jane Marple, knitting away in her village cottage or on shipboard or in various exotic settings, is one of Agatha Christie Mallowan's two most famous detectives. Miss Marple's simple soul conceals a sharp wit, intelligence, and a gift for observation under her English country gentlewoman exterior. She provides her detective friends (and relatives) with insights into crimes based on her acute observations of village life and her ability to relate that knowledge to the crime at hand. It does seem, however, that it would be dangerous to live in her neighborhood— more murders were committed in her immediate vicinity than occurred in all of England in a year. As a matter of fact, the same holds true for all fictional detectives. They attract murders the way black suits attract lint.

4. d. Hercule Poirot, the little Belgian (*not* French) detective, was Agatha Christie's other most famous detective. He has a large head, a foreign (as conceived by Miss Christie) turn of phrase, and some unusual mannerisms. He said, for example, "It gives one furiously to think," which does not translate into a French

phrase at all, but certainly indicates that his mother tongue was not English.

5. g. Inspector Maigret was the all-too-human character created by Georges Simenon, French by birth, Swiss by residence. The books featuring the country-born French inspector are beautifully constructed psychological novels with deep philosophical insights. An interesting sidelight on the difference between French and English (or American) detective stories is that Inspector Maigret takes the Metro (subway) frequently. British and American detectives commandeer squadcars or drive their own, but Maigret can be found meditating on the Metro in most of Simenon's books about him. He lives on the Boulevard Richard Lenoir, and he gets off at a real Metro stop. Simenon uses real street names and real restaurant and bistro names, and there is hardly a writer who can evoke Paris life more convincingly. Anyone who knows Paris can follow Maigret down the street and call up a visual image of exactly where he is. Simenon has also been lucky in his translators, who have caught his rather elliptical style very well indeed. Madame Maigret has also developed a life of her own. She is described as a housewife who cooks extremely well—one enterprising publisher brought out quite a good cookbook featuring her recipes.

6. o. Nero Wolfe and Archie Goodwin, the ill- or well-matched pair, depending on how you look at it, were the brain-children of Rex Stout. Nero Wolfe is the immensely fat (a quarter of a ton, according to Stout) gourmet, orchid fancier, and detective, and Archie Goodwin is the foil who does Wolfe's footwork. Wolfe expresses disgust and annoyance at many subjects but analyzes everything that Archie digs up in his inquisitive, private-eye style. In contrast to Maigret, who lives modestly in a walk-up flat, Nero Wolfe resides in a private brownstone in New York City, complete with rooftop orchid greenhouse, elevator, and all of the other appurtenances of fine living, including a resident chef, Fritz. Fritz has followed Madame Maigret down the culinary path to fame, with *The Nero Wolfe Cookbook*. The name was Nero Wolfe's, but the recipes were Fritz's.

7. m. Steve Carella is a member of a large metropolitan police force

in the United States. (The city sounds like New York.) Using the pen name Ed McBain, Evan Hunter, the creator of this strong police procedural series, has created a varied and interesting group of detectives, who represent, far more than in any other series, the wide ethnic diversity of a metropolis. These books usually center around one particular episode, but often contain unresolved subplots.

8. h. The very large detective, Dr. Gideon Fell, is the creation of John Dickson Carr. These stories were extremely popular when they first came out, despite the fact that they are not all genuine detective or mystery stories.

9. e. Albert Campion was the very British hero delineated by Margery Allingham (Mrs. Philip Youngman Carter). He first appeared in 1929, and, never aging in accordance with the passing years (detectives rarely do), he thought his way through a series of adventures, the most famous of which was *The Fashion in Shrouds,* which is one of the few detective stories in a couture setting, with a clever convoluted plot, and a believable cast of characters, stirred into an interesting mixture, with a glimpse into a very different life-style.

10. b. John Creasey, the one-man British detective story factory, turned out a whole series on Inspector Roger West, a pleasant, harassed family man who is also a big wheel in the London police. These are actually procedural novels, with many threads being woven simultaneously into a rich tapestry of London life and crime. They are well plotted and full of detail and character. Creasey succeeds rather well in making West a genuine person. He has foibles, likes, dislikes, and a believable family. There are many, many subplots, some of which are wound up, some of which are not (in preparation for the next book, which usually continues the subplot), and the picture of police life is excellent.

11. a. J. J. Marric (one pen name of John Creasey) is the author of the Commander George Gideon series of police procedurals, *Gideon's Day, Gideon's Week, Gideon's Year,* and others. Creasey-Marric seems to have written more than six hundred books during his prolific career and also seems to have run out of ideas for original titles.

12. j. G. K. Chesterton's Father Brown appeared in numerous short stories. Father Brown solved his problems and the mysteries with a combination of thought, religion, and a strange blend of cynicism and innocence. The stories are interesting, but quite dated.

13. l. The rakish figure of the Saint, his halo set at an angle, was thought up by Leslie Charteris (Bowyer Yin), who is also one of Mensa's more famous members. Almost a dozen books were written about this dashing debonair figure (who bears a fairly close physical resemblence to his author), and many, many short stories. The Saint, whose real name is Simon Templar, lives by his wits. Charteris's stories might be considered more adventures than detective stories, but can, with some stretching, be included in this category. These too seem quite dated now—flippant, wisecracking, very much of the 1930s, when they were written.

14. f. This well-born sleuth, socially the highest-ranking detective of the lot, was a brother of the current holder of a dukedom. Dorothy Sayers originally portrayed him as a bit of a fop, a rather silly-seeming person, who hid his wits under that disguise. In later books, however, Sayers developed his character more fully, and his intelligence began to show. Sayers was a graduate of Oxford, and the setting for several of the books is Oxford and its colleges. Wimsey's wife, Harriet Vane, may be modeled on Sayers. A Sayers biography is titled *A Very Strange Lady,* which she was. Her religious conversion later in life led to the publication of several books dealing with philosophy and religion. Lord Peter has also been the hero of two television series.

15. k. The chief charm of the Bill Knox series starring Webb Carrick is their setting. Webb Carrick is an officer in the Fisheries Protection Service, and spends his life aboard a small, fast boat tracking down fish poachers, intruders, and other nefarious characters. On the way, he stops at small ports, where murder frequently occurs, and solves the murders and mysteries while protecting fisheries. Bill Knox paints a vivid picture of life in the small fishing villages along the Scottish coast and its islands. The hard, rather cheerless landscape, the self-sufficiency of the population, and the adherence to many of the old folkways of life are clearly described.

16. n. Roderick Alleyn is a high-ranking police officer, married to a gifted artist, who has a sidekick and assistant, whom he calls Br'er Fox. He is the creation of the New Zealand writer Dame Edith Ngaio Marsh. His adventures take place in some exotic locales, like sheep ranches, and are interesting not only for the plots, which are well done, but for the glimpses of a life and a country not well known to many.

II.

1. Mycroft Holmes was Sherlock's older brother, and Sherlock Holmes claimed many times that his brother was cleverer than he. Mycroft's hobby was beekeeping. He belonged, according to Holmes, to the Diogenes Club, about which absolutely nothing is known except its name.

2. Sherlock Holmes had previously lived in Montague Street, near the British Museum, as reported by Dr. Watson. Unlike 221B Baker Street, this address has not become a shrine.

3. The French painter Vernet was a relative of Holmes's grand-mother, and Holmes once stated that she was Vernet's sister. He was proud of his French blood—he said it provided him with valuable insights.

4. This is a subject of debate. In one story, Watson speaks of being wounded in the shoulder. In another, he refers to himself as having a bad leg from a war wound. Although never mentioned in the stories, it is, of course, entirely possible that he was wounded more than once.

5. "The Woman," as Holmes always referred to her, was Irene Adler. She was involved in an adventure with the king of Bohemia. Holmes had a framed portrait of her on display. Other than this one woman, there is no discussion of any woman whatsoever in Holmes's life, except for his landlady. He was singularly unattached to anyone.

6. The "Speckled Band" was an Indian viper, extremely poisonous, and the means by which the wicked stepfather, Dr. Roylott, murdered Miss Stonor's sister. It should be noted that the surviving Miss Stonor could not have been very astute. The story states that

her bed was fastened to the floor so that it could not be moved, and there was a false pull descending from a ventilator. Holmes noticed these interesting details immediately when he saw the room. Miss Stonor, who lived in the room, had not noticed these singular features. This plot detail requires the willing suspension of disbelief.

7. *A Study in Scarlet* is based upon a rather lurid account of the Mormons (Latter-Day Saints). It is a sensational story of murder, revenge, and a lifelong search for the two men who had committed crimes against the girl John Hope had loved. At the end the newspapers gave all the credit to Gregson and Lestrade of Scotland Yard, the two detectives who appear in this and other early stories but gradually disappear.

8. In "The Adventure of the Devil's Foot," which is set in Cornwall, Holmes and Watson ingest a bit of the suspected toxin used for a murder and begin to hallucinate. Doyle provides an excellent description of such hallucinations, which undoubtedly owes a lot to his medical training.

9. Dr. Watson married Mary Morstan, the heroine of "The Sign of (the) Four." She apparently died between the original death of Sherlock Holmes and the publication of his subsequent adventures. Dr. Watson may have married again—there is some allusion to it—but no hint as to his second wife's name is ever given.

10. Doyle had studied in Edinburgh and often stated that his model for Holmes was Dr. Joseph Bell of the Edinburgh Infirmary. The doctor was a genius in the art of diagnosis.

11. The stories were illustrated by Sidney Paget, the most famous of the illustrators who drew Holmes. He showed Holmes in the cloak and the signature deerstalker hat that now identify him instantly. It is of interest to note that the famous hat—now a trademark—is never mentioned in the stories. The popular image of Holmes is based on Paget's illustrations, not Sir Arthur Conan Doyle's descriptions.

CHAPTER 5

What Was It Originally?

Many masterpieces in English literature were not originally English at all. We rarely think of *Hedda Gabler,* for example, as a Norwegian play, so firmly is it a part of the literary tradition whenever playwriting and drama are studied.

This is true of many, many other literary works. Cervantes's *Don Quixote* has added a picaresque tale to the worldwide literary canon, as well as adding an adjective to the English language.

This same is true of characters in fiction. Robinson Crusoe is very well known. His "original," Alexander Selkirk, he ran away to sea in the late seventeenth century and was put ashore on an uninhabited island when he declared his vessel was unseaworthy. Selkirk was right; it sank, and he spent more than four years on the island before being rescued. How many of us know Alexander Selkirk? How many Robinson Crusoe?

Other important literary characters have been based on real people. Do you know who they are? Are you fascinated by a roman à clef? Do you have the key to many of them? If not, you may add to your store of knowledge in this area as some well-known personages are here asked for and identified.

Happy identification!

I.

Each of the following books, plays, novels, or short stories was originally published in a language other than English. On the left is a list of the works with titles in the original language, on the right a list of the authors. Match them up and provide the English titles of the various works. Some, of course, have slightly different titles, depending upon the translator, but even these minor variations are readily recognizable.

1. *Le Médecin malgré lui*

2. *Notre Dame de Paris*

3. *Keisjerens nye klaeder*

4. *Domroscher*

5. *Grande et inestimable Chronique du Grand et Énorme Géant Gargantua*

6. *Il Principe*

7. *À la recherche du temps perdu*

8. *La Peste*

9. *Cien Años de Solidad*

10. *La Condition Humaine*

a. Jacob Ludwig and Wilhelm Carl Grimm

b. André Malraux

c. Albert Camus

d. Jean-Baptiste Molière

e. Victor Hugo

f. Hans Christian Andersen

g. Marcel Proust

h. Gabriel García Márquez

i. François Rabelais

j. Niccoló Machiavelli

II.

*We have had books under names that may be unfamiliar and titles
that do not appear in English. Now there are characters also in
disguise. The fictional character or characters are listed on the left.
The list on the right contains the names of the individuals on whom
the fictional characters were based or (supposedly) modeled. Match
them up, then give the title of the book or other literary work in
which the characters appear and the author's name.*

1. Meg, Jo, Beth, and Amy

2. D'Artagnan

3. Richard Hannay

4. Henry Higgins

5. Joe Egg

6. Sir John Falstaff

7. The Darlings, including
   Wendy

8. Dr. Pangloss

9. Marie Roget

10. Madame Bovary

a. Marie Cecilia Rogers

b. The Alcotts: Elizabeth, May,
   Anna, and Louisa

c. John, Michael, John Michael,
   and Sylvia Davies

d. Delphine Delamare

e. Adrian Gilbert

f. Baron Gottfried Wilhelm
   Leibniz

g. Charles de Baatz

h. William Edmund Ironside,
   Field Marshal Lord Ironside
   of
   Archangel

i. Henry Sweet

j. Abigail Nichols

III.

*This is a simple substitution cryptogram, based on a
(misspelled) word.*

QUJP ANKFFKO JHE QCR PFKQCX QITRP EKE OXNR
JHE OKGAFR KH QCR UJAR JFF GKGPX URNR QCR
AINIOITRP JHE QCR GIGR NJQCP ISQONJAR

IV.

To solve a quotation puzzle, use the letters at the bottom of each column to fill in the squares at the top of that column. The letters have been arranged alphabetically. A letter will be used once for each time it appears so cross off each letter as you use it. Black squares indicate word ends. Words may begin on one line and continue on the next.

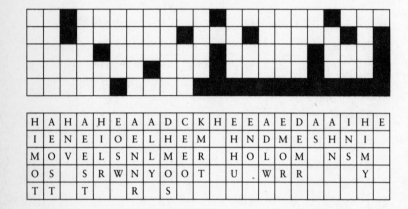

ANSWERS

I.

1. d. *Le Médecin malgré lui* is known in English as *The Physician in Spite of Himself,* written by Molière. The so-called doctor is actually a maker of faggots for wood burning, who is called in to cure the daughter of a neighbor after his wife tells the neighbors he is really a doctor but won't admit it unless they beat him well. (This is in revenge for a beating he has given her.) He cures the girl by bringing in her lover, disguised as an apothecary.

2. e. Victor Hugo's novel is better known in English as *The Hunchback of Notre Dame.* This romance of medieval times, featuring the hunchback Quasimodo and the gypsy girl Esmeralda, is a tragedy. Esmeralda is finally executed as a witch, after being denounced by the evil Archdeacon Frollo. Quasimodo throws Frollo to his death from the bell tower of Notre Dame and everything ends unhappily ever after.

3. f. Hans Christian Andersen wrote *The Emperor's New Clothes,* along with 167 other fairy tales, not to mention poetry, plays, and novels.

4. a. *Sleeping Beauty* has been reprinted in dozens of fairy-tale anthologies and was made into a classic animated feature by Walt Disney. The Grimm brothers enjoyed long and distinguished careers, separately and together. They were eminent philologists and achieved permanent fame in linguistics with Grimm's Law, a description of consonant changes over the course of time in various languages.

5. i. Rabelais wrote the satire *Gargantua and Pantagruel.* Gargantua is a legendary giant (whose name has passed into the language —there is even a food store in Paris called Gargantua). Gargantua is noted for his voracious and insatiable appetite. When he was a baby, nearly eighteen thousand cows had to be milked to supply his daily food. The book is considered a satire on the Reform Party by some and on the court of Francis I by others. Fortunately, the King apparently did not see it as such, or Rabelais would have disappeared into a prison somewhere, possibly permanently.

6. j. Machiavelli wrote *The Prince* as a guide to ruling and using power. Machiavelli's name has come to be synonymous with cunning and possibly deceitful manipulation. The basic theme of *The Prince* is that rulers may resort to any action, provided the end justifies the means. But Machiavelli also believed in unity and that good government was possible.

7. g. Marcel Proust's novel, *Remembrance of Things Past,* could be better translated as *In Search of Lost Times.*

8. c. Albert Camus's masterpiece, *The Plague,* deals with an outbreak of bubonic plague in Oran, Algeria. Written shortly after World War II, Camus's dark absurdist novel was partially a response to the horror of the Holocaust and anti-Semitism.

9. h. This is *One Hundred Years of Solitude* by Gabriel García Márquez. It is one of the best and most well-known examples of magic realism.

10. b. André Malraux wrote *Man's Fate,* known by its rather different French title, in 1933. (In England the book was called *Storm over Shanghai.*) All of Malraux's early books dealt with Communism, of which he was a staunch supporter until World War II. The books are, most critics feel, more than the usual revolutionary fiction. Malraux later became a bitter anti-Communist and wrote *Man's Hope* on the subject.

II.

1. b. Louisa May Alcott was the author and the model for Jo, second of the four March sisters. The others were modeled after Alcott's sisters. Her sister May illustrated the first edition of *Little Women,* which related their story. Elizabeth, who was Beth in the novel, did indeed die young, at age twenty-three, and her death is recorded touchingly in the novel, as are the scrapes into which Jo got herself. Apparently, Louisa May Alcott was indeed a rather tomboyish but literary person herself. Jo is the best-drawn, most sympathetic of the heroines in the book.

2. g. Alexandre Dumas, *père,* was the author of *The Three Musketeers.* The hero, D'Artagnan, together with Athos, Porthos, and

Aramis, was the epitome of the brave not-too-sophisticated mus-keteer. D'Artagnan was modeled on Charles de Baatz, Seigneur D'Artagnan, a soldier from Gascony who served at the French court. The other musketeers were also based on real people. Though their exploits were fiction, the names of the characters were real.

3. h. John Buchan wrote the Richard Hannay novels, most notably *The Thirty-Nine Steps* (which Hitchcock made into a superb movie). The original of Hannay, the dashing and fearless hero, was apparently Field Marshal Ironside, who spoke fourteen lan-guages, held a decoration from Germany, which he earned while serving behind the German lines as a British spy, and had many other remarkable exploits to his credit. Ironside was not particu-larly well liked, but was made a field marshal and a Lord under Winston Churchill. It was said, rather unkindly, that he was kicked upstairs, as he retired once he had received all these hon-ors. On the other hand, he was sixty at the time. Ironside was 6-feet 4-inches tall (hardly inconspicuous as a spy) and was noted for going up the Home Office steps three at a time.

4. i. George Bernard Shaw indicated that the character of Professor Higgins from *Pygmalion* (and then *My Fair Lady,* its musical adaptation), was based on Henry Sweet, a philologist who died in 1912. *Pygmalion* was written in 1913.

5. j. Peter Nichols wrote *A Day in the Death of Joe Egg* based upon his own experiences with his badly handicapped child, Abigail, who died at eleven after spending almost all her life in an insti-tution. Nichols was heartsick and wounded by this badly afflicted child, and turned his personal problem into a moving and tender play.

6. e. Shakespeare is supposed to have used Adrian Gilbert, younger brother of Sir Humphrey Gilbert, as his model. According to some authorities, Shakespeare first called his character John Old-castle, but this turned out to be the name of a martyr whose family objected to the use of the name. Gilbert was described as a very heavy buffoon. He was also given to deer poaching and dabbled in medicine.

7. c. James M. Barrie became a great friend of the Davies family, and when John Michael and Sylvia both died in their early forties, he became the guardian of their children. Wendy is a name that Barrie made up—it did not exist as a girl's name prior to the appearance of *Peter Pan*, but has become popular subsequently. Barrie got the name from W. E. Henley's infant daughter, who called Barrie *friend*, but could not pronounce the word. Sadly, she died in very early childhood.

8. f. In *Candide*, Voltaire modeled Dr. Pangloss on the philosopher Baron Gottfried Wilhelm Leibniz. Voltaire spoofs Leibniz's optimism by having Pangloss fatuously profess, "All is for the best, in this best of all possible worlds."

9. a. Edgar Allan Poe knew Marie Cecilia Rogers and the tobacco shop where she worked. When her body was found in the Hudson River, the story of *The Mystery of Marie Roget* suggested itself to him. Incidentally, the Rogers murder was never solved. The man believed to be responsible was later executed for another crime, so perhaps justice was served.

10. d. Delphine Delamare was the very young (seventeen years old) wife of a much-older country doctor. She became a devotee of romance novels, ran up debts trying to be like their heroines, and acquired lovers, also apparently in imitation of fiction. She committed suicide at twenty-six, and her husband then killed himself. The husband had been a pupil of Dr. Flaubert, the novelist's father.

III. The code was based on the word JABBERWOCKY. It was not possible to use the two *b*s because of the need to use each letter only once. The alphabet runs as follows:

```
J A B E R W O C K Y D F G H I L M N P Q S T U V X Z
A B C D E F G H I J K L M N O P Q R S T U V W X Y Z
```

TWAS BRILLIG, AND THE SLITHY TOVES DID GYRE AND GIMBLE IN THE WABE, ALL MIMSY WERE THE BOROGROVES, AND THE MOME RATHS OUTGRABE.

IV. TO SHERLOCK HOLMES SHE IS ALWAYS THE WOMAN. I HAVE SLEDOM HEARD HIM MENTION HER UNDER ANY OTHER NAME.

ART (TK--????)

CHAPTER 6

Plot and Counterplot

Legend says there are only two or three basic plots, endlessly repeated. One writer even named a play after Plot Number 1: *Boy Meets Girl*. But, of course, the plots of books and dramas are as varied as life itself. There are as many plots as there are human experiences.

I.

Ten plots from actual literary works are outlined below. Many of these are about other subjects than love—not that love isn't well represented. But other themes also exist, and this is a fair sample of some of the other ideas available. The characters involved in the plots have been identified as "a" or "b" and so on. Your literary puzzle is to fill in the names of the characters, and give the title and author of the work.

1. A successful but stingy businessman (a) has in his employ a young—relatively young, that is—clerk (b) who is cheerful, optimistic, and the father of a large family. Among his children is a fragile child (c) who needs expensive care that the poor clerk cannot provide. The rich old miser did have a partner (d) at one time, but the partner died. The miser falls asleep and his partner's ghost returns to visit him. He tells the miser he is wandering the earth in search of comfort because of his lack of charity during his life. Meanwhile, the poor clerk and his

family are preparing to dine, not too well, but happily. The wicked old miser sees the future, has a change of heart, rewards the clerk, takes care of the sick child, and is a changed human being—changed for the better, happily, as it would be hard to see how he could change for the worse. _____

2. An aristocratic but poor woman (a) is saddled with debts on her family estate, and the estate is about to be sold. Her daughter (b) is in love with a young revolutionary student, who is of no help in this crisis, so busy is he foreseeing a new order for his country. A rich but humbly born neighbor (c) suggests that they sell the most prized portion of the property for suburban building lots, which would enable them to pay off all their debts. In a telling comment on the aristocracy, they do not do so. They keep waiting for "something to turn up." Nothing occurs to save them, the estate is sold for debt, and, crowning the whole problem, the rich neighbor who has advised them to sell for building lots buys the property at the debt sale and does exactly that. _____

3. An American (a) involved with an American widow (b) whom he is going to marry, goes to Europe to bring home her wandering and errant son (c). The son seems to be more concerned with having a good life abroad than with returning to his responsibilities at home in Massachusetts. The emissary from his mother finds that the son is having an emotionally satisfying life in Europe, where he is romantically involved with a charming and delightful lady. The son feels that he is living a life that would not be available to him in Massachusetts, and that he is living life to the fullest. (Parenthetical note—this is obviously someone with a fairly large private income—a great help in living a rich, full life without working). The young man's sister also arrives to lead him firmly back to the path of duty, but also

to no avail. She does not like the life abroad and fails completely to see its attraction for her brother. Eventually, all the Americans, except the young man, return to the United States, unsuccessful in their mission, and the young man remains to enjoy his idyllic life in Europe.

4. A young man (a) comes to a tuberculosis sanitarium to visit a relative, but upon discovering that he himself is ill, stays there for seven years. This is a symbolic novel, whose characters include a beautiful, exotic Russian woman (b). There is also a character representing the practical (c) who tries to recall the young man to his everyday life and release him from the nearly magical spell of the sanitarium. He undergoes a spiritual experience during a snowstorm in which he gets lost—symbolizing his failure to find his way in more-or-less metaphysical snowstorms. He recovers and is last seen going into battle with a Schubert song on his lips, apparently having learned to live with both the practical and the spiritual sides of his nature. This novel, considered one of the most important works of the twentieth century, is one of the most striking in its plot, symbolism, and vividly drawn scenes and images.

5. The eponymous heroine of this novel (a) is a rich, unoccupied young lady who, out of the goodness of her heart, meddles officiously and unsuccessfully in the affairs of her friends and acquaintances. She encourages a young, poor orphan (b) whom she has befriended to look, as the British would say, "above her station," and the young girl is rebuffed. The other romance she tries to bring about is also a failure. Then the young orphan decides she is interested in the heroine's brother-in-law (c), a pleasant man fifteen years older than the heroine, and the heroine decides that she really loves him herself. The heroine encourages the orphan to

marry her original fiancé, a young farmer, and the heroine marries her brother-in-law herself. This novel is one of the best illustrations of the rather rigidly drawn class distinctions of that time. _____

6. The unnamed heroine who cannot be identified by a letter except as her husband's wife (a) comes with her husband (b) back to his magnificent family home, where she is greeted, but not welcomed, by the housekeeper who was devoted to her husband's now dead first wife. There are dark hints of murder, and the new wife finally learns that the first wife (c), using the name of the housekeeper (d), had visited a specialist and learned that she was dying. She had taunted her husband by telling him she was going to have another man's child and had then died under mysterious circumstances. When all appears to be turning out well, the housekeeper evidently sets fire to the mansion, which is destroyed, leaving second wife and husband to pursue their lives elsewhere. _____

7. A time machine, in the form of a blow to the head, makes a New Englander (a) awaken in A.D. 528. His shrewdness and modern common sense reconstruct the time in which he finds himself. He saves himself from execution by remembering that an eclipse occurred on the day that has been set for his execution and predicting it—his jailers are duly impressed when the eclipse occurs. He marries a young woman of the times, and they have a daughter whom he names after the telephone system he has installed (b), but the powerful magician of the time (c) plots the hero's downfall. Eventually, the magician brings about the New Englander's return to the present (his present), and he is bereft of his wife and daughter. _____

8. This novel was one of the first, if not the very first,

to use the stream-of-consciousness technique. It gives, via various technical devices, a view of a day in the life of three main characters (a, b, c), following them and their movements in a major city. The day is June 6, 1904.

_____

9. This novel, in seven books, was first published in another language, but has become famous in an English translation. Basically, there are three separate groups or individuals in this plot. There are two families (a and b), representing the aristocracy and the nouveau riche, and an individual, a young man, representing the established bourgeoisie (c). There is also the narrator (d) as seen by the young man. The novel describes thoughts, ideas, memories, and also real events, like various social gatherings in the three levels of society described. There are also frank discussions and descriptions of homosexual affairs, which made its acceptance somewhat difficult in this country. The Dreyfus case plays an important role in this particular set of books, with the narrator being a Dreyfusard and suffering because of it. The anti-Semitism of much of the French upper class is clearly shown in this description of the Dreyfus case.

_____

10. This epic poem relates the story of a hero (a) who goes on a long journey and has difficulty returning home. The various books of the poem relate his adventures along the way and his final return to his wife (b), who does not recognize him. She has managed to fend off suitors who believed her to be a widow (as she did herself), by setting impossible tasks to be accomplished to win her. When the hero returns, he accomplishes the tasks, they recognize each other, and there is a happy ending. The title of the book means the "wanderings of the hero" and has become a generic term for long and difficult journeys.

_____

II.

The line below has characters from Charles Dickens in it. They have been "interleaved," but all the letters are in the proper order. Unscramble the characters.

L M A M I R T R T I N C M I T H U C L Z A W E Z
L B N E W E E I R L T L

III.

The following word square has a quotation coiled in it. Start at the correct letter and move in any direction to an adjacent letter to find the quote. The author's name is also included.

T A H H I A T P E R

A N T H S H H D E C

R P E T S H H O T C

I W I H W O C T U E

L L E R U H R H A R

O S S E G T A E C H

O T E D U E M R E X

E T H R O O F O O T

IV.

Which of the following names is odd man out? One of these, when unscrambled, does not match the others. Which one is it?

E R L W O M A

S N O N O J

E W D L I

W H A S

B T U N R O

ANSWERS

I.

1. This is Charles Dickens's *A Christmas Carol,* and (a) is Scrooge, the famous miser and misanthrope. His name is now a synonym for a greedy, avaricious, stingy individual. Bob Cratchit is (b), the relatively young, cheerful clerk who tries to look on the bright side although he is underpaid and overworked. Cratchit is married, has several children, and among them is a little boy, Tiny Tim (c), a fragile child who obviously needs good medical attention, which the Cratchits cannot afford. They are almost preternaturally cheerful in the face of the grinding poverty. Several of the Cratchit children are working, but they do not have money enough for anything except the bare necessities of life. Scrooge's partner was Marley (d). It is actually his ghost which plays such a prominent role in the story, preparing Scrooge for the arrival of the ghosts of Christmas past, present, and future. Scrooge sees the error of his selfish ways, and all ends happily. The more than 150-year-old story is still a Christmas classic.

2. Anton Chekhov's play *The Cherry Orchard* is set in Russia in the few years immediately preceding the Russian Revolution. Mme. Lubovanreyevana Ranevskaya is a formerly rich landowner, an aristocrat. The land she owns is heavily burdened with debt, and she does nothing about it, trusting that something will occur to save her fortune. Her daughter Anya (b) is in love with a young student, obviously part of the new wave of Russian reform that was to erupt into revolution in less than ten years. The young student represents the new generation of Russians who do not care for rank and privilege but want a more democratic society. The neighbor Lopakhin (c) is a rich but humbly born peasant, who has made money in rather unscrupulous ways. His humble birth makes Madame totally unwilling to listen to his advice. He suggests selling the large cherry orchard to a speculator interested in building lots for suburban houses, but she rejects the idea completely. Of course, in the end, the neighbor buys the land when it is up for auction, and goes ahead with the plan to sell the cherry orchard. The story is a commentary on the blindness of the aristocrats to the fact that changes are coming. It is apparent

that many Russians saw the cataclysm coming, but that most of the aristocrats and nobles, including the royal family, simply shut their eyes and pretended that if they didn't notice the problems they would go away. This is a stunning portrait of a society on the brink of disaster.

3. Henry James's *The Ambassadors* contrasts the culture and luxury of life in Europe with the spartan simplicity and Puritan ethos of Massachusetts. Lambert Strether (a) is intending to marry a wealthy widow, Mrs. Newsome (b). She has a happily married, conventional daughter and a son, Chad (c), whom she regards with deep distress because he has gone to France to live, and is obdurate in his refusal to return home. Mrs. Newsome feels he should return and accept his responsibilities, so she sends her fiancé off as her ambassador to Chad, to persuade him to return. Strether finds Chad very happy in France. He is involved with a beautiful and intelligent woman, Countess de Vinoet, and thoroughly enjoying life as an expatriate. He has been accepted into French society (no mean feat) and is enjoying the cultured life of this class. Chad's sister and brother-in-law also come to Europe to try to persuade him to come home. They, unlike Strether, see nothing admirable or enjoyable in the upper-class life of wealthy Europeans, and exhort Chad about his duty. Strether and Chad's family eventually return to Massachusetts, but Chad remains in France. It should be noted that this story may well be a reflection of James's own feelings about the attractions of America and Europe. James grew up and was educated in Europe and New York. He became a naturalized British citizen during World War I. The novel contrasts philosophies and life-styles between the French—or, European—upper classes and the same class in the United States, which James saw as crass and materialistic.

4. *The Magic Mountain,* by Thomas Mann, is considered one of the most important novels of this century. This is an allegorical novel, showing man in conflict with himself. The hero, Hans Castorp (a), finds himself in a sanatorium for seven years, and meets the exotic Clavdia Chauchat (b), who represents the sensual and romantic ideals of life. The practical, exemplified by Mynheer Peeperkorn (c), tries to present the life of sense and rationality. Castorp struggles with the various warring aspects

and, while not resolving them, does manage to return to the real world, apparently at least partially reconciled to the disparate elements in his nature.

5. *Emma* is considered one of Jane Austen's most psychologically interesting novels, although not her most popular or best known. Emma (a), the heroine, befriends the young Harriet Smith (b), who has turned down a nice young farmer who wished to marry her. Harriet has succumbed to Emma's subtle promise that she can do better than the farmer for a husband. Emma sees depths and virtues in Harriet that are not apparent to others. Emma encourages her to believe that the clergyman loves her. In fact he is grossly offended when he learns of this, as Harriet is far below his station in life, and he returns to the village with an upper-middle-class wife who is polished but extremely boring. Emma then encourages a romance between two other characters, one of whom is secretly promised to a third person. The meddling is therefore unsuccessful. When Harriet decides she has fallen in love with Emma's brother-in-law, Mr. Knightly, the bachelor brother of her sister's husband, Emma discovers that she wants to marry him herself. She does, and the young farmer, happily for Harriet, returns to claim her as his wife.

6. In the novel *Rebecca*, by Daphne Du Maurier, the heroine is never called anything except Mrs. De Winter (a). She returns with her husband, Max (b) (actually named Maxim), to the home he had occupied with his first wife, Rebecca (c). The housekeeper, Mrs. Danvers (d), was intensely devoted to the first Mrs. De Winter. It appears at one point as though Max may have murdered his first wife—she had taunted him that she was expecting a child by another man. Actually, she had learned that she was going to die very shortly. When the house, Manderley, is destroyed by fire, the heroine and her husband look forward to a life free from the past—and from Mrs. Danvers, who has disappeared. This was made into a remarkably successful movie.

7. *A Connecticut Yankee in King Arthur's Court*, written by Mark Twain, is not a comedy. It is a satire on the inability of the average citizen to adapt to anything new, even when it is for his benefit, and also on the general ignorance of the relationship

between wages and prices. The common folk complained bitterly about high prices in their area compared to another section, and the Yankee hero (a) was unable to convince them, for example, that since their wages were twice as high, they would have to expect to pay twice as much for goods. The book is full of other such examples. The hero, who wakes up in King Arthur's Court after a blow on the head, tries to introduce schools and telephone service—he names his little daughter Hello Central (b). However, Merlin (c) takes advantage of the Yankee's temporary absence from court and sends him back to his own time.

8. *Ulysses* by James Joyce was a milestone in the history of English literature. It apparently introduced the "stream of consciousness" pattern, wherein the thoughts of the character are not orderly, but rather fragmented and jumbled, as thoughts often are, interrupted, broken by irrelevant ideas, and in general more true to actual life than to literary tradition. *Ulysses* follows Stephen Daedalus (a), Leonard Bloom (b), and Molly Bloom (c) through a day in Dublin. The book is broken into sections, which copy the pattern of the *Odyssey* of Homer. For example, in Part XVIII, Molly is Penelope, waiting for her wandering husband. The book required seven years to finish, and was, when published, the center of heated and bitter court battles. *Ulysses* was not legally admitted into the United States until 1934, although it had been published, in sections, in a magazine, prior to 1920. It was attacked as both obscure and unintelligible, and also as obscene—the apparently contradictory nature of these accusations not seeming to trouble the people who made them. The novel is now recognized, along with *Finnegans Wake* and *Dubliners*, especially the latter, as a major influence on twentieth-century literature.

9. Marcel Proust's *Remembrance of Things Past* concerns the Guermantes (a), the Verdurins (b), and Charles Swann (c), the hero. The narrator is Marcel, who describes the others—and his relationship with his family and friends. This is a "portrait parle" of French society and is amazingly frank, as it is in its depiction of homosexuality.

10. Déjà vu. The poem is *The Odyssey*, the famous classical history of the Trojan War and its aftermath, and Ulysses (a) is the hero

of the title. It is done in the format of many "books," a format copied by James Joyce. Each details one theme or one series of adventures of Ulysses on his long voyage back to his wife, Penelope (b). When he finally arrives at home, he wins a contest and is thus recognized. *Ulysses* is the prototype of the long epic poem and one of the first in recorded history. Its name can refer to any long series of wanderings or journeys.

II.

LITTLE NELL   MARTIN CHUZZLEWIT   MR. MICAWBER

III.

WHEN THAT APRILLE WITH HIS SHOURES SOOTE THE DRAUGHTE OF MARCH HATH PERCED TO THE ROOTE . . . CHAUCER. (Start at W in middle)

IV.

The odd man out is the last, BURTON. The others were all dramatists: MARLOWE, JONSON, SHAW, AND WILDE; BURTON was an actor.

CHAPTER 7

Colors, Numbers, and Kids

This chapter contains literary trivia or, if you will, odd questions about books, plays, and other literary material.

I.

Here, an author's name is given. You are requested to fill in the title of a work by that author that has a color in the title. One example would be The Red Badge of Courage *by Stephen Crane.*

1. Stendhal   _____

2. Robin Moore   _____

3. Kingsley Amis   _____

4. Marc Connelly   _____

5. Anna Sewall   _____

6. Joseph Wechsberg   _____

7. Alice Walker   _____

8. William Henry Hudson   _____

9. Charles Perrault   _____

10. Maurice Maeterlinck   _____

11. James Fenimore Cooper   _____

12. Sir James Frazer   _____

13. Herman Melville   _____

14. Alan Moorehead   _____

15. Henry Steele Commager _____

II.

The same thing can be done with numbers that appear in titles. Here is a list of titles. This time, you give the authors.

1. *Three Men in a Boat* _____

2. *Twenty Thousand Leagues Under the Sea* _____

3. *The Four Million* _____

4. *Four Saints in Three Acts* _____

5. *The 42nd Parallel* _____

6. *Seventeen* _____

7. *Ninety-Three* _____

8. *Twenty Years After* _____

9. *Two Years Before the Mast* _____

10. *A Tale of Two Cities* _____

11. *The One-Hoss Shay (The Deacon's Masterpiece)* _____

12. *Ten Days That Shook the World* _____

13. *The House of the Seven Gables* _____

14. *Tales of the Five Towns* _____

15. *The Thirty-Nine Steps* _____

III.

While the category of biographies differs from those above, the format is the same. Each of the following people wrote a famous biography. Your pleasant puzzle is to name the person who was written about. (In some instances, the writer published several biographies—any of them will do).

1. James Boswell   _____

2. Samuel Eliot Morrison _____

3. Parson Weems (Mason Locke Weems) _____

4. Henry Adams _____

5. Ernest Jones, M.D. _____

6. Robert E. Sherwood _____

7. Lytton Strachey _____

8. Lady Antonia Fraser _____

9. Carl Sandburg _____

10. Irving Stone _____

IV.

While we all have different experiences and backgrounds, there is one thing we all have in common. We were all children once. The readers of this book should be familiar with some of the classics for children that have been written and published in the nineteenth and twentieth centuries. Here is a description of plots. Give the author and the title of the book.

1. This imaginative tale relates the stories of several animals living in The Forest. Among them are Eeyore and Wol (aka Owl), the only literate character. Also involved in the adventures was an ursine creature that more or less belonged to the human child protagonist, or perhaps it was the other way around. These characters also appeared in a sequel, in two books of poems, and eventually in Walt Disney movies.

_____

2. This book of life on a river includes Mole and Water Rat. It was written as a bedtime story for the author's son, but has since become a classic of children's literature.

_____

3. In this fantasy tale, a poor and orphaned chimney sweep, through a series of misfortunes, falls into the water. Although his body is drowned, he is transformed into another creature that lives in the water. Eventually, the young girl who befriended him hits her head on a rock and dies. She too is transformed into a water creature, and after many tribulations and adventures the two are symbolically saved. Although a fairy tale of sorts, this story has a strongly evangelical twist, and Tom, the poor chimney sweep, is eventually allowed to go to Heaven, where his little girlfriend goes on Sunday, but where he is originally not allowed to accompany her.

_____

4. Max, a small boy, has misbehaved and is sent to bed without supper. He fantasizes himself into the place where untamed creatures roam, and has many adventures with them. Eventually, he decides he wants to go where somebody loves him and returns to his own home, where he finds supper waiting for him.

_____

5. The little girl heroine lives in a log house in Kansas, far, far from any other families or any town. The book describes the adventures of the girl and her family in their isolation in the wide open spaces of the West.

_____

6. The grandson of an English earl, whose father was disinherited for marrying beneath his station, becomes heir to the title and goes to live in England. After the boy endears himself to his grandfather and everyone else, an impostor shows up and is finally revealed as such, to everyone's great relief.

_____

7. A pet pig is saved from being turned into bacon by the small daughter of the house, but the pig knows he will eventually meet his fate. A little gray spider, through a series of remarkable interventions, saves him.

   _____

8. The story of a young boy who runs away from a brutal father and the "civilizing" influence of society. He befriends a runaway slave and they have numerous adventures. This is a sequel to an earlier book in which the boy is a secondary character.

   _____

9. The hero, a rabbit dressed in human clothes in the charming illustrations, strays into the garden of a testy Scotsman. He is caught, but escapes, leaving some of his clothes behind, and rejoins his mother and three sisters safely at home.

   _____

10. The hero is sent to the British public school Rugby, where he meets Dr. Thomas Arnold, the famous headmaster. He gets into various schoolboy scrapes. After he leaves the school, he returns to attend Dr. Arnold's funeral, where he has what the author indicates is a religious conversion experience.

    _____

V.

The following terse verse has a coiled sentence at the end. When you uncoil it, the rhyme will be completed. Start at any letter in the coiled sentence box, and move in any direction to find the ending, which will rhyme. (One null letter.)

THE GRIMM BROTHERS MIGHT NOT NECESSARILY
APPROVE:
ONCE UPON A TIME, MARKED THEIR FAIRY TALE

T	M	O	E	Y	A	L
H	E	D	A	Q	V	E
X	E	R	D	U	I	N
I	N	N	E	M	A	T
K	S	T	H	L	I	T
I	C	E	H	C	E	H

ANSWERS

I.

1. The Stendhal book is *The Red and the Black*. This 1830 novel is a strong psychological study of Julian Sorel, a selfish, egotistical young man. The colors are those of Napoleon, whom Stendhal admired greatly, and of the clergy (black) whom he detested, and represent the two paths open to a young man of Julian's class.

2. The book is *The Green Berets*, a story of combat in Vietnam, which was immensely popular during that war.

3. This is *The Green Man*, a modern novel, rather bitter and satirical as are all of Amis's books.

4. Marc Connolly is the author of the immensely successful Pulitzer Prize-winning play *The Green Pastures*. It is a black preacher's retelling of the Bible in terms of the familiar daily round of the lives of his congregants. No one who saw it will ever forget the opening, when a stentorian voice announces "Make way for the Lord God Jehovah."

5. The story of *Black Beauty* has been a favorite for years. It was required reading for many years in schools and it pleads for better treatment of animals. The whole title is *Black Beauty, His Grooms and Companions*.

6. This noted food writer produced *Blue Trout and Black Truffles,* a classic on eating, food, the good life, and the author's early life in Europe. It is a mouth-watering collection of essays on gastronomic pleasures, with plenty of philosophy and humor mixed into the verbal stew.

7. *The Color Purple*. This novel by Walker is a moving and poignant portrayal of black life. It received critical acclaim and was also a popular success.

8. The chef d'oeuvre of William H. Hudson was *Green Mansions*, starring Rima the Bird Girl, who understands the language of the wild things in the forests of South America. The story is told in the first person, has a tragic ending, and was a bestseller for years.

9. *Little Red Riding Hood* was one of the tales collected by Charles Perrault (1697). It has become a classic of the fairy tale genre.

10. Maurice Maeterlinck's drama *The Blue Bird* deals with the search for the Blue Bird of Happiness by the two children of a woodcutter. It ends with the Blue Bird escaping, with the moral that it is impossible to catch the Blue Bird of Happiness.

11. *Red Rover* is an atypical James Fenimore Cooper book. It describes the exploits, not of Indians or settlers, but of a sea pirate who finally sees the error of his ways and serves the United States during the Revolution.

12. *The Golden Bough,* which refers to the branch broken from a sacred tree by Aeneas, is a major work in the history of anthropology, comparative religion, folklore, and legend. It appeared in twelve volumes between 1890 and 1915 and is still considered the definitive work of its kind.

13. *White Jacket* was one of Melville's better-known works, all of which dealt with life at sea or in the islands of the South Pacific. His most famous work, of course, is *Moby Dick,* or *The White Whale.*

14. *The Blue Nile,* a book, obviously, about Egypt, is the work of Alan Moorehead.

15. *The Blue and the Gray* was Commager's epic work about the Civil War, or The War Between the States. It is considered a classic of its time.

II.

1. Jerome K. Jerome wrote this classic bit of humor more than one hundred years ago, but it is still in print. Jerome is possibly best known for his successful play, *The Passing of the Third Floor Back.*

2. This is one of Jules Verne's science fiction masterpieces. In it, Captain Nemo conveys his submarine around the world far, far under the sea. Even those who never read the book are apt to know the story and something of the plot, as it has been made

into an amusement ride at the Walt Disney parks. On the ride, the visitor descends into a submarine that runs on tracks, and travels under the water of a small artificial lagoon. All kinds of special effects are provided to give the sensation of truly being far under the sea, although the apparatus is actually barely covered.

3. This is O. Henry's collection of stories about New York, when that city had only four million inhabitants. It is full of satirical, witty, wry stories, usually with a twist in them and a surprise ending, which was this author's hallmark.

4. *Four Saints in Three Acts* was written by Gertrude Stein in her usual rather incomprehensible style, in which not the words, but the sounds, were meant to convey meaning. It was not a success, either critically or popularly. Virgil Thompson set it to music, which may prolong its life.

5. This is the first novel of John Dos Passos's famous trilogy, *U.S.A.* (the others are *1919* and *The Big Money*). It is a picture of the United States just before World War I and was strongly influenced by the author's sympathy for Marxist beliefs, which he later renounced. It also includes biographies, in capsule form, of many of the most famous men of the day.

6. Booth Tarkington wrote *Seventeen*, a story of adolescence. The kinds of problems facing teens of those times were very different from today, but Willie Baxter is the eternal adolescent who is not quite sure how to grow up. *Seventeen* was made into both a musical comedy and a motion picture.

7. This Victor Hugo novel about events in 1793 deals with the perils lurking in wait for three little children. It contains excellent descriptions of several famous revolutionary characters.

8. The later life of the characters in the musketeer series is outlined and described in *Twenty Years After* by Dumas. The musketeers are older, but not much wiser.

9. Richard Henry Dana wrote this famous narrative of his experiences on a sailing ship that went around Cape Horn, the southernmost part of South America, a region noted for extremely

dangerous storms. Dana was only twenty-two when he made this voyage and the book that came out of it made him famous.

10. *A Tale of Two Cities,* by Charles Dickens, was inspired by the French Revolution. The French Revolution was a major theme in early nineteenth century literature because it was an upheaval of what had looked like a stable and enduring form of government. Dickens was not particularly enamored of the Revolution. The most unpleasant characters in the book are revolutionaries, including Madame Defarge.

11. *The One-Hoss Shay,* the title of which is really *The Deacon's Masterpiece,* by Oliver Wendell Holmes, Sr., was an elocution staple for children in the days when children took elocution lessons. The poem relates the tale of a carriage, built so well that it lasted for a hundred years and then disintegrated into dust, totally and completely, in one instant.

12. This book by John Reed, published in 1919, was extremely sympathetic to the Russian Revolution. It told the story of the revolution in most laudatory terms. This was one of the first books by an American intellectual to praise the new regime in Russia.

13. This almost Gothic novel by Nathaniel Hawthorne deals with the tortuous evolution of the revenge upon the Pyncheon family. An ancestor of the Pyncheons had condemned a man to death on witchcraft charges, knowing the charge to be false. The condemned man had cursed the family of his judge and its heirs. The complex plot, dealing with several generations of Pyncheons and Maules (the man who had been executed), finally resolves itself with the marriage, centuries later, of a descendant of each family.

14. Arnold Bennett wrote this collection, *Tales of the Five Towns.* His most famous work though, is probably the novel, *The Old Wives' Tale.* The towns are the Potteries district of England, where pottery has been made for centuries. Bennett disguised the towns very thickly, but they are easily recognizable.

15. This is one of the classic adventure-suspense-spy novels of John Buchan. This one is set pre-World War I, with the brave and courageous Richard Hannay as the hero. The book was made into a superb movie by Alfred Hitchcock.

III.

1. James Boswell was the biographer of the great lexicographer Dr. Samuel Johnson and wrote the *Life of Samuel Johnson*. This work is considered a model biography and details, in scrupulous minutiae, those incidents and words that reveal Johnson's personality and character. Additional papers of Boswell's were found in Malahide Castle, in England, tucked away in a trunk that had not been opened for over 150 years. A devoted American nearly bankrupted himself acquiring the papers, so that additional volumes of Boswell's *Life* could be published. The first volume appeared in 1791, the second in the mid-twentieth century.

2. Morrison wrote *Admiral of the Ocean Sea*, published in 1942, about Christopher Columbus. He received the Pulitzer Prize for this complete in-depth portrait of a controversial and complex man. He wrote other biographies but none received a Pulitzer Prize except this one.

3. Parson Weems was the biographer of George Washington. He wrote several volumes, revising as he went, and it was in the fifth edition that the story of the young Washington chopping down the cherry tree first appears. It has now passed into folklore and semi-official history.

4. Henry Adams was his own biographer, in the book *The Education of Henry Adams*. Adams, who won a Pulitzer Prize for this work, a companion piece to his famous *Mont-Saint Michel and Chartres*, saw himself as a cultured individual battling a cruel and hostile world. He was a genuine pessimist and the book portrays, gloomily, the decline of the society in which he lived.

5. Jones published the authoritative three-volume life of Sigmund Freud. The book is still considered the most definitive and complete work on Freud, but controversy swirled around Jones after the book was published.

6. *Abe Lincoln in Illinois,* awarded a Pulitzer Prize, was probably the finest work of playwright Robert E. Sherwood, who was also a speechwriter for FDR. Many of his plays, like *Tovarich* and *Idiot's Delight,* were popular as well as critical succcesses.

7. Lytton Strachey achieved fame for his biography of Queen Victoria. This was a relatively sympathetic portrait. He was also well known for his biography *Elizabeth and Essex.*

8. *Mary, Queen of Scots* is the best known, probably, of Lady Antonia Fraser's various works. Lady Antonia is known for her meticulous research and complete accuracy of detail, while painting the character in broad, recognizable strokes. Take credit also for naming any of her other biographies, of Cromwell, for example, or any of many other outstanding characters from English history.

9. Sandburg's best-known biography is that of *Abraham Lincoln.* It is an exhaustive (and exhausting) study of Lincoln, the man and the statesman, published in six volumes. It won the Pulitzer Prize in 1940.

10. Irving Stone's best-known work is probably *Lust for Life,* the biography of Vincent Van Gogh. He also wrote *The Agony and the Ecstasy,* about Michelangelo.

IV.

1. The famous series of Winnie-the-Pooh stories featured A. A. Milne's son, Christopher Robin, as the hero. These wildly popular books, including *Now We Are Six* and *When We Were Very Young,* are delightfully illustrated in the original editions by Ernest Shepherd. It is of interest that the translation of *teddy bear* was not entirely accurate. In several places the bear is referred to as Edward, the British using Teddy as a nickname for Edward. But the real teddy bear's full name was Theodore. Milne was apparently unaware that the Teddy Bear was named in honor of Theodore Roosevelt.

2. *Wind in the Willows,* written by Kenneth Grahame as a bedtime story for his young son, achieved fame, but Grahame never wrote anything like it again. Grahame was a troubled and unhappy man who wanted great things for his son, who was born with very poor eyesight. The boy, whom Grahame adored and cherished, died in mysterious circumstances in his late teens. Grahame apparently never wrote anything again, but he will live in children's literature for a long time for this particular book. It has become a generation-spanning classic.

3. This is *Water Babies* by Charles Kingsley. Tom is drowned while running from pursuers who falsely accuse him of theft, but is turned into a "water baby," which the illustrations show to be a tiny baby that lives underwater. It is a semireligious tract, but charming and appealing nonetheless.

4. This is Maurice Sendak's *Where the Wild Things Are*. It is clever, imaginative, and wholesome and has appealed to at least two generations of children. Since Max eventually goes home to find that all is forgiven, children can heave a sigh of relief at the end.

5. Laura Ingalls Wilder wrote *The Little House on the Prairie*, and several other books relating an autobiographical story of life on the frontier wilderness. She calls the heroine Laura, but writes in the third person, not the first. The books spurred a television series.

6. This is Frances Hodgson Burnett's most famous book, *Little Lord Fauntleroy*. The golden curls, velvet suit, and endearing ways of this saccharine youngster made him beloved of everyone, according to Mrs. Burnett. Perhaps this should be classed as a fairy tale, not simply a fiction.

7. *Charlotte's Web*, by E. B. White, with its highly unlikely heroine, a spider, and its equally unlikely hero, a piglet, has delighted children for many years now. The theme is rather frightening— the hero is about to be made into pork chops and bacon—but all comes out right in the end.

8. This is *Huckleberry Finn*, the companion piece to *Tom Sawyer*, with a slightly better-known plot. It is in the tradition of the picaresque novel.

9. Peter Rabbit, in *The Adventures of Peter Rabbit* by Beatrix Potter, was almost caught in Mr. McGregor's garden, where his father had been captured and made into rabbit pie, but he escaped safely and went home to Flopsy, Mopsy, Cottontail, and their mother. After the author married at nearly fifty, she never wrote again, fully adopting the life of a farmer's wife.

10. *Tom Brown's Schooldays*, by Thomas Hughes, is the most famous story of British public school life, and it is also rather

moralizing, as were most books for children in the nineteenth century. It conveys a very favorable picture of the famous Dr. Arnold and a clear picture of life at such a school.

V.

THE MODERN DAY EQUIVALENT: THE CHECK IS IN THE MAIL.

CHAPTER 8

What's in a Name?—Shakespeare, to Be Exact

The facts of Shakespeare's life are somewhat obscure. First, we don't really know the date of his birth. We know the date of his christening, the date of his marriage to Anne Hathaway, and that he (probably) had three children. We have a death record for his son, a marriage record for one of his daughters, and some town records, but no really good evidence exists to help us determine the exact number of children he had. We know he moved to London and secured the patronage of the Earl of Southampton, to whom he dedicated "Venus and Adonis," but we know almost nothing about the identity of some of the other people to whom the plays and other works were dedicated. We have Shakespeare's will, dated March 25, 1616, and we know he died on April 23, 1616. His tomb still stands and is inscribed with a verse by Ben Jonson.

There are some contemporary comments about Shakespeare's plays, but not many. We have contemporarily published copies of his plays, but public records in Shakespeare's time were not so thorough as they are now and the only information about anyone of that time is pretty much limited to court documents, military dispatches, or diplomatic correspondence. Parish registers, yes; land-owning records, yes; stories about an individual, no.

We do have, however, a complete set of the thirty-eight plays generally accepted as the work of Shakespeare. (Please do not write me long, reasoned discourses on the fact that Shakespeare did not write the plays and other works credited to him. We are assuming, for this book, that Shakespeare wrote Shakespeare. Whether or not he did is the subject of another book.)

I.
Match the name of the character in one of Shakespeare's works with the play.

1. Berowne		a.	*Henry V*
2. Count Paris		b.	*Troilus and Cressida*
3. Leonato		c.	*A Midsummer Night's Dream*
4. Parolles		d.	*The Merry Wives of Windsor*
5. Imogen		e.	*Love's Labour's Lost*
6. Bolingbroke		f.	*Romeo and Juliet*
7. Anne Page		g.	*Much Ado About Nothing*
8. Sir Thomas Erpingham		h.	*Cymbeline*
9. Hermia		i.	*All's Well That Ends Well*
10. Cassandra		j.	*Richard II*

II.
Shakespeare took his inspiration from Greek and Roman mythology, from legends and history, from other literature, and from earlier plays. He used some very different locales for his plays. Following is a list of the locales in ten of the plays. Some of these locations appear elsewhere in a play, but each of the locations is described as given in the stage direction. Athens and London, for example, appear in several plays but not exactly as described here.

1. The palace of the duke

2. The palace of the king of Sicily

3. The queen's palace in Alexandria, Egypt

4. An "open place" in Scotland

5. The battlements of a castle

6. Padua

7. Vienna, Austria

8. On board a ship, probably off Italy

9. Ephesus

10. The antechamber of the king's palace in London

a. *Hamlet*

b. *The Comedy of Errors*

c. *Measure for Measure*

d. *The Winter's Tale*

e. *The Taming of the Shrew*

f. *Macbeth*

g. *The Tempest*

h. *A Midsummer Night's Dream*

i. *Antony and Cleopatra*

j. *Henry V*

III.

As the college student said, he liked Shakespeare, but his works were too full of quotations. It's true. Shakespeare and the Bible contain the most quoted lines in English. Ten slightly less-well-known quotations from Shakespeare are given here. Give the play, and if you can, the speaker.

1. I must go seek some dewdrops here,
   And hang a pearl in every cowslip's ear.

2. How sharper than a serpent's tooth it is
   To have a thankless child!

3. First thing we do, let's kill all the lawyers.

4.   She never told her love,
   But let concealment, like a worm i' the bud,
   Feed on her damask cheek. She pined in thought,
   And with a green and yellow melancholy,
   She sat like Patience on a monument,
   Smiling at grief.

5.   Then must you speak
      Of one that loved not wisely but too well,
      Of one not easily jealous, but, being wrought,
      Perplexed in the extreme; of one whose hand,
      Like the base Judean, threw a pearl away
      Richer than all his tribe . . .

6. Oh, my offense is rank, it smells to Heaven.
    It hath the primal eldest curse upon't,
    A brother's murder.

7. Why, there was a crown offered him; and being offered him, he
    put it by with the back of his hand, thus. And then the people fell
    a-shouting.

8. Once more unto the breach, dear friends, once more;
    Or close the wall up with our English dead.

9.   In such a night
      Stood Dido with a willow in her hand
      Upon the wild sea banks and waft her love
      To come again to Carthage.

10. Never. He will not.
    Age cannot wither her, nor custom stale
    Her infinite variety. Other women cloy
    The appetites they feed, but she makes hungry
    Where most she satisfies. For vilest things
    Become themselves in her, that the holy priests,
    Bless her when she is riggish.

IV.

*Each of the following three puzzles contains a quote from
Shakespeare. To solve these puzzles, use the letters at the bottom of
each column to fill in the squares at the top of that column. The
letters have been arranged alphabetically. A letter will be used once
for each time it appears, so cross off each letter as you use it. Black
squares indicate word ends. Words may begin on one line and
continue on the next.*

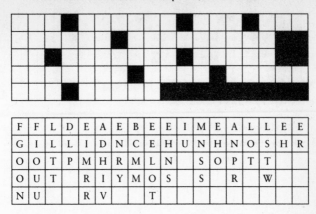

F	F	L	D	E	A	E	B	E	E	I	M	E	A	L	L	E	E
G	I	L	L	I	D	N	C	E	H	U	N	H	N	O	S	H	R
O	O	T	P	M	H	R	M	L	N		S	O	P	T	T		
O	U	T		R	I	Y	M	O	S		S		R		W		
N	U			R	V			T									

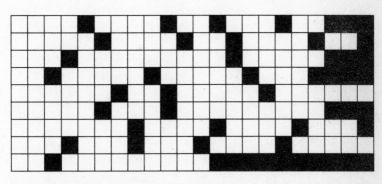

G	F	A	A	A	E	A	E	A	A	M	B	E	A	E	E	E	A	L	E
H	H	E	A	H	M	D	E	A	I	A	N	E	E	E	H	H	D	G	A	S	S
N	I	E	D	H	N	D	I	D	N	D	O	L	M	E	N	I	N	L	I	S
O	O	M	H	H	N	G	M	E	R	I	S	M	M	I	N	R	O	L	I	V
S	O	O	S	I	N	I	M	H	S	P	S	R	S	J	N	S	O	R
T	O	S	T	I	O	M	R	S	W	O	T	Y	S	L	O	W	S	T
T	O	T	T	L	S	U	S	T		S	U		T	W		T
T	R		N		T		Y		S	U
W	T

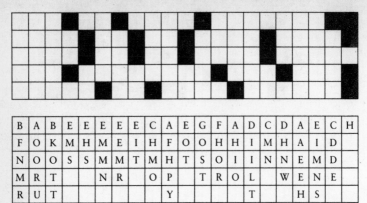

B	A	B	E	E	E	E	C	A	E	G	F	A	D	C	D	A	E	C	H
F	O	K	M	H	M	E	I	H	F	O	O	H	H	I	M	H	A	I	D
N	O	O	S	S	M	M	T	M	H	T	S	O	I	I	N	N	E	M	D
M	R	T			N	R		O	P		T	R	O	L		W	E	N	E
R	U	T						Y				T			H	S			

ANSWERS

I.

1. e. Berowne appears in *Love's Labour's Lost,* which does not seem to have been written for the stage. There is some internal evidence that it was written for a party or reception at the home of the Earl of Southampton. This is sometimes adduced as the reason for Southampton's patronship of Shakespeare. The style is quite florid, far more so than that of many of the other plays, and could be explained by the fact that it was written for a far more educated and cultured audience than Shakespeare could expect to attend his stage plays.

2. b. Paris is the other suitor for the hand of the lovely Juliet. However, her father, at the time Paris presses his suit, believes Juliet to be too young. He states plainly that she is not yet fourteen. This is the only instance in which the girl's age is given, so we are definitely aware that Juliet is only a child, despite the fact that children were often married at this age.

3. g. *Much Ado About Nothing* is a delightful comedy, set in Messina, Sicily. Leonato is the governor of Messina, and the play starts with a messenger announcing the arrival of Don Pedro, prince of Aragon. The Silicians had been ruled for five hundred years by a king of Aragon, after they overthrew the French rule. The name of the prince who is coming to Messina is the same as that of the historical king of Aragon, but the play has no historical significance. There is no evidence that anyone in the play is a real person, despite several similarities in names.

4. i. *All's Well That Ends Well* is a comedy that owes much of its plot to one of the tales in Boccaccio's *Decameron*. Parolles is the favorite friend of Bertram, the young Count of Rousillon. Rousillon is in France, just north of the Pyrenees. Rousillon, although French in the play, was actually part of Aragon until 1465, but the play proceeds as if it were permanently and genuinely French. This isn't exactly true, as Rousillon was shuttled between France and Spain until 1650, when it became permanently French. So, when Shakespeare was writing, it was actually Spanish, a fact that he ignores.

5. h. Imogen is the name of Cymbeline's daughter. This comedy takes place in England, theoretically at the same time as *Antony and Cleopatra*. Much of early British history is lost in the mists of preliteracy but there is some evidence that a king named Cymbeline lived in the first century B.C.

6. j. Bolingbroke is talked about in several of the plays, but he appears in *Richard II*. Bolingbroke is deeply involved with the plots and counterplots of this complicated story—which is no more complicated than the actual history.

7. d. *The Merry Wives of Windsor* has several plot lines dependent upon Anne Page and her large dowry of seven hundred pounds. (In today's money, that would be about $700,000.)

8. a. Sir Thomas was apparently an old comrade of Henry V. The king meets him during the fourth act and gives him the honor of opening the battle the next day.

9. c. In *A Midsummer Night's Dream*, Hermia is the daughter of Egeus, who is trying to make her marry Demetrius (who is actually in love with Helena, who loves him), and not Lysander, who loves her and is loved in return. Demetrius, however, does appear to want to marry Hermia. The complications of this delicious plot get as convoluted as an audience can be expected to follow.

10. b. Cassandra was Priam's daughter. A vengeful Apollo, to whom she had reneged on a promise, gave her the gift of prophecy, but added the proviso that she would never be believed: She was thought mad. You would think that after half-a-dozen prophecies had come true, she would have been listened to with a little more attention, but the curse held true. In *Troilus and Cressida*, she warns the raiders that Helen must be returned to Troy, but naturally, no one listens.

II.

1. h. *A Midsummer Night's Dream* takes place partially in the palace of the duke of Athens.

2. d. *The Winter's Tale* is supposed to take place in Sicily.

3. i. *Antony and Cleopatra* starts in the palace of the queen in Alexandria, Egypt. This play is based on known history and the characters are reasonably close to their real-life counterparts, in contrast to many plays where the only thing the characters share with their namesakes are their names.

4. f. The Scottish heath where *Macbeth* opens is the setting for the scene of the three witches. Of interest to trivia collectors: this is the only witchcraft in all of Shakespeare's plays.

5. a. It is still possible to walk on the battlements of Elsinore Castle in Denmark and *Hamlet* is performed there during summer drama festivals.

6. e. The "play within a play" in *The Taming of the Shrew* takes place in Padua. In the prologue, the hero sits down to watch a play, and this is it.

7. c. *Measure for Measure* is set in Vienna. Although the scene is described as Austria, all the characters have Italian names, probably from the same sort of mental fixation that makes paintings of the time depicting Biblical themes have Italian backgrounds, however inappropriate.

8. g. *The Tempest* starts on board a storm-tossed ship, a challenge to today's stage directors as it must have been to stage directors back in those days.

9. b. The play may well have been Shakespeare's first production. *The Comedy of Errors* is derived from a play by Plautus, the Roman dramatist, *Menechini*. Both plays tell the tale of two brothers separated at birth and the resulting mistaken identities as the twins grow up.

10. j. *Henry V* opens in the year 1414. Two high Church officials are discussing a law which, if passed, will have major consequences for the Church. In 1414, the country was still Catholic, and Shakespeare, writing 150 years later, following the split of the English Church from Catholicism, expected his audience to understand the law's importance. There may have been those in the audience who lived through Henry VIII's change of ecclesiastical rule.

III.

1. *A Midsummer Night's Dream,* Act II, Scene i, l. 14–15. This is said by one of the fairies in the train of the Fairy Queen.

2. *King Lear,* Act 1, Scene iv, l. 310–311. This is King Lear himself speaking of his daughters, Regan and Goneril, who prove to be ungrateful.

3. *Henry VI,* Part II, Scene iv, l. 86. This has often been used as a weapon against lawyers, but it is not so meant in the play itself.

4. *Twelfth Night,* Act II, Scene iv, l. 113–118. These lines are recited by Viola, disguised as Cesario. She pretends she is speaking of her sister and tells her love to Orsino.

5. *Othello,* Act V, Scene ii, l. 343–348. This often quoted piece is spoken by Othello, not in justification of his murder of Desdemona, but merely as an explanation as he is taken away to be tried.

6. *Hamlet,* Act III, Scene iii, l. 36–38. Hamlet's uncle, who has murdered his brother, Hamlet's father, and married his brother's wife, kneels to pray in deep remorse.

7. *Julius Caesar,* Act I, Scene ii, 1. 220–221. Casca is explaining why Caesar has a peculiar look upon his face. These lines point out that Caesar had refused the crown that was offered to him in front of the Roman mob, hoping that they would force him to accept it, so that he could claim to be King (Emperor) by popular acclamation. Instead, he was cheered for refusing the crown. Casca says his ploy turned on itself.

8. *Henry V,* Act II, Scene i, lines 1 and 2. These lines are spoken by Henry V himself, to boost the sagging spirits of his troops.

9. *The Merchant of Venice,* Act V, Scene i, l. 9–12. Lorenzo's speech is one of frequent references to this particular legend in the works of Shakespeare.

10. *Antony and Cleopatra,* Act II, Scene ii, l. 239–245. The description, of course, is of Cleopatra, and is one of the most telling portraits of a seductive woman ever written. Enobarbus is assur-

ing some of the other characters that Antony will never leave Cleopatra, and gives the reasons in this much-admired and often-quoted speech. (Incidentally, *riggish* means "wanton.")

IV.

NOT MARBLE NOR THE GILDED MONUMENTS OF PRINCES SHALL OUTLIVE THIS POWERFUL RHYME.

GOOD NAME IN MAN OR WOMAN, DEAR MY LORD, / IS THE IMMEDIATE JEWEL OF THEIR SOULS: / WHO STEALS MY PURSE STEALS TRASH; / TIS SOMETHING, NOTHING; / TWAS MINE, TIS HIS, AND HAS BEEN SLAVE TO THOUSANDS;

BUT HE THAT FILCHES FROM ME MY GOOD NAME / ROBS ME OF THAT WHICH NOT ENRICHES HIM, / AND MAKES ME POOR INDEED.

CHAPTER 9

Other Voices, Other Styles

Many authors have a style all their own. It is unique; they speak in their own voice, and it is possible to identify their works without much difficulty. The writing style is as distinctive as a voice heard over the telephone. If you are familiar with the style, it is unmistakable. Some, indeed, have a style that can be, and is, easily parodied.

The following selections are not parodies but the actual work of the authors. Identify the authors. If you can spot the work also, good for you.

I.

1. The doubleviewed seeds. Nun, lemmas quatsch, vide pervoys akstiom, and I think as I'm suqeez in the limon, stickne punctum, but for semenal rations I'd likelong, by Araxes, to mack a capital Pee for Pride down there on the batom[1] where Hoddum and Heave, our monsterbilker balked his bawd of parodies. And let you go, Airmienious, and mick your modest mock Pie out of Humbles up your end. Where your apexojesus will be a point of order. With a geing groan grunt and a croak click cluck.[2] And my faceage kink and kurkle trying to make

105

keep peep.[3] Are you right there, Miachel, are you right. Do you think you can hold on by sitting tight?

[1] Parsee ffrench for the upholdsterer would be delighted.
[2] I'll pass out if the screw spliss his strut.
[3] Thargam then goeligum? If you sink, I can, swimford. Suksumkale!

_____

2. The sun came through the upon window and shone through the beer bottles on the table. The bottles were half full. There was a little froth on the beer in the bottles, not much because it was very cold. It collared up when you poured it into the tall glasses. I looked out of the open window at the white road. The trees beside the road were dusty. Beyond was a green field and a stream. There were trees along the stream and a mill with a water wheel. Through the open side of the mill I saw a long log and a saw in its rising and falling. No one seemed to be tending it. There were four crows walking in the green field. One crow sat in a tree watching. Outside on the porch the cook got off his chair and passed into the hall that led back into the kitchen. Inside, the sunlight shone through the empty glasses on the table.

_____

3. Proud of my broken heart since thou didst break it.
Proud of the pain I did not feel till then.
Proud of my night since thou with moons dost slake
   it.
Not to partake thy passion, my humility.

_____

4. He made no answer: but began pacing the room with an irresolute air as if he were undecided whether to remain or depart, and as if he had some quarrel with himself for being there at all. But soon his tread grew slower and heavier, and his face more sternly thoughtful; as the object with which he had come, fixed itself into his mind and dilated there again.

While he thus walked up and down with his eyes on the ground, Mrs. ____, in the chair from which she had risen to receive him, sat listening anew. The monotony of his step, or the uncertainty of age, made her so slow of hearing, that a footfall without had sounded in her daughter's ears for some moments, and she had looked up hastily to warn her mother of its approach, before the old woman was roused by it. . . .

5. The pandemonium of delight which turned itself loose now was of a sort to make the judicious weep. Those whose withers were unwrung laughed till the tears ran down; the reporters, in throes of laughter, set down disordered pot hooks which would never in the world be decipherable and a sleeping dog jumped up, scared out of its wits, and barked itself crazy at the turmoil. All manner of cries were scattered throughout the din. "We're getting rich." . . .

6. Wondering and bewildered by words she could not comprehend, but excited even to tears by the plaintiveness of their tone, . . . listened these outpourings of a full and oppressed heart. In truth, A. . . . himself was softened much beyond his ordinary mood, which to outward seeming was usually either sullen or impetuous. For the noblest desires are of a jealous nature . . . they engross, they absorb the soul, and often leave the splenetic humours stagnant and unheeded at the surface. Unheeding the petty things around us, we are deemed morose, impatient at earthly interruptions to the divine dreams, we are thought irritable and churlish. For as there is no chimera vainer than the hope that one human heart shall find sympathy in another, so none ever interpret us with justice; and none, no not our nearest and our dearest ties, forbear with us in mercy! When we are dead and repentance comes too late, both friend and foe may wonder to think how little there was in us to be forgiven!

7. How far, since then, the ocean streams
   Have swept us from that land of dreams,
   That land of fiction and of truth
   The lost Atalantis of our youth.   _____

8. Of these States the poet is the equable man.
   Not in him but off from him things are grotesque,
       eccentric, fail of their full returns,
   Nothing out of its place is good, nothing in its place
       is bad.
   He bestows on every object or quality, its fit pro-
       portion,
   Neither more nor less.
   He is the arbiter of the diverse, he is the key.   _____

9. For always the fervid languid glories
   Allured of heavier suns in mightier skies
   Thine Ears knew all the wandering watery sighs
   Where the sea sobs round Lesbian promontories.
   The barren kiss of piteous wave to wave
   That knows not where is that Luecadian grave.   _____

10. The youngest son did not often come home, either,
    but when he came, it was always to tell of some
    success he had made, and he told of it, laughing
    and proud, and he grew vain of his success and his
    luck, and he came to believe that luck was his be-
    cause he had some favor of Heaven. He would
    boast, "Heaven chose me to that work," or he said,
    "To that place Heaven led me," or he said,
    "Heaven put power in my hand," until one day [his
    father] burst out, "Do not say Heaven this and
    Heaven that! I tell you what happens on earth now
    is not the will of Heaven. It is not Heaven's will
    that men kill each other, for Heaven created us. If
    we must kill, then let us not say it is Heaven who
    bids it!" This he said as a father may speak to a
    son, and he was not pleased when he saw his hand-
    some son lift his lip at him and sneer at him.   _____

11. Vic cursed him.

     "I'm telling you, Mr. Vic, a country girl wouldn't sit on a high step in front of a man, not when she wasn't wearing nothing but that blue wrapper, anyhow."

     "Shut up," Vic said, laying the steelyard down on the quilt beside him.

     The man under the water oak closed the blade of the small knife and put it into his pocket. The big cowhide-covered knife he flipped into the air and caught easily on the back of his hand.

     "What's your name?" he asked Willie. _____

12. And if you vote for truth I think you will someday
     look on me with gratitude
     For having called your attention to the verities of
     the platitude.
     No paradox of Mr. Chesterton's ever contained the
     amount of validity
     Contained in the simplest statement that It's not
     the heat it's the humidity;
     Wilde and his epigrams are shown up as brilliant
     bores
     Before the unpretentious penetration of the com-
     ment that When it rains, it pours. _____

13. When all my fine and country senses see,
     The fingers will forget green thumbs and mark
     How, through the halfmoon's vegetable eye
     Husk of young stars and bandfull zodiac
     Love in the frost is pared and wintered. _____

14. But then they danced down the street like dingle-
     dodies, and I shambled after as I've been doing all
     my life after people who interested me, because the
     only people for me are the mad ones, the ones who
     are mad to live, mad to talk, mad to be saved,
     desirous of everything at the same time. _____

15. One of my great-grandfathers (and x's), for an admittedly juicy example was a quite famous Polish-Jewish carnival clown named Zozo, who had a penchant—up to the very end, one necessarily gathers—for diving from immense heights into small containers of water. Another of (x's) and my great-grandfathers, an Irishman named Mac-Mahon (whom my mother, to her everlasting credit, has never been tempted to refer to as a "darlin' man"), was a self-employed type who used to set out a couple of octaves of empty whiskey bottles in a meadow and then, when a paying crowd had closed in, dance, we are told, rather musically on the sides of the bottles.

II.

Just as writers have distinctive voices, writers with a common interest, who share a common set of ideas and are contemporaries, frequently influence each other. In many instances, they are close friends, and the style of each writer is sometimes subtly influenced by the criticism or suggestions of such comrades in pen (or typewriter, or word processor). Following is a list of famous writers. A second list, of a group of associates, is given opposite. Match the famous writer with his (or her) friends.

1. Virginia Woolf

2. William Wordsworth

3. Percy Bysshe Shelley

4. Dante Gabriel Rossetti

5. William Shakespeare

6. Alfred, Lord Tennyson

7. Friedrich Nietszche

8. Theodore Dreiser

9. George Bernard Shaw

10. Stephen Spender

a. C. Day Lewis, W. H. Auden

b. H. L. Mencken, Arnold Bennett

c. Lytton Strachey, E. M. Forster, the Sitwells

d. The Fabian Society, Sidney Webb

e. Samuel Taylor Coleridge, Sir Walter Scott, Thomas DeQuincey

f. Leigh Hunt, George Gordon, Lord Byron, William Hazlett

g. Algernon Swinburne and George Meredith

h. Edward FitzGerald, Edward Lear, Coventry Patmore

i. Christopher Marlowe and Ben Jonson

j. Richard Wagner

III.

Here are ten works by non-English-language writers, the translations of which have become famous. In some instances, the translators have also become famous. Match work and translator. These are not necessarily the only translations, but they are the most famous ones.

1. *The Rubaiyát of Omar Khayyám*

2. Anthelme Brillat-Savarin, *The Physiology of Taste*

3. Christopher Columbus, *Journal of the Third Voyage*

4. *The Divine Comedy*, by Dante Alighieri

5. Marcel Proust, *Remembrance of Things Past*

6. *Cyrano de Bergerac*, by Edmond Rostand

7. *Waiting for Godot*, by Samuel Beckett

8. Count Leo Nikolayevich Tolstoy, *War and Peace*

9. Guillaume de Loris and Jean de Meun, *Le Roman de la Rose*

10. *The Magic Mountain*, by Thomas Mann

    a. Samuel Eliot Morison

    b. Edward FitzGerald

    c. C. K. Scott-Moncrief

    d. H. Wolfe

    e. Samuel Beckett

    f. Constance Garnett

    g. Geoffrey Chaucer

    h. Dorothy L. Sayers

    i. M. F. K. Fisher

    j. H. T. Lowe-Porter

IV.

*There is another group of writers who all share one characteristic:
the writers who have won the Nobel Prize for Literature. Authors,
of all nationalities, who have won the award are listed on the left.
The author's country of origin or residence is on the left. Match
them.*

1. Odysseus Elytis, 1979
2. Maurice Maeterlinck, 1911
3. Hermann Hesse, 1946
4. Frans E. Sillanpää, 1939
5. Halldór K. Laxness, 1955
6. Saint-John Perse, 1960
7. Gabriel García Márquez, 1982
8. Wole Soyinka, 1986
9. Miguel Angel Asturias, 1967
10. Ivo Andríc, 1961
11. Pablo Neruda, 1971
12. Naguib Mahfouz, 1988
13. Nelly Sachs, 1966 (shared)
14. Shmuel Yosef Agnon, 1966 (shared)
15. Luigi Pirandello, 1934

a. Switzerland
b. Italy
c. Greece
d. Yugoslavia
e. Belgium
f. Iceland
g. Sweden
h. Colombia
i. France
j. Israel
k. Finland
l. Guatemala
m. Nigeria
n. Chile
o. Egypt

V.

The following quotation has been encoded, using the name of the editor-author-collector as the code word. The name of the author of the quotation is at the end. To make this short quote just a little bit harder, it has been broken up into groups of five letters, so that you must find word divisions also.

```
B W J S F      T G S U H      N P Q H A      N H P V A
G A I P O      E W H Y B      H P V A I      J O Q P Q
S A Q H P      I W H Y B      H P V A J      I A U P Q
J x x x x
```

ANSWERS

I.

1. This is James Joyce at his most Joycean in *Finnegans Wake*. The passage illustrates his late style very clearly—the made-up words, the jesting and incomprehensible footnotes, the flow of language.

2. This is Ernest Hemingway's *An Alpine Idyll*. Hemingway's is a very easily copied style, and many have parodied it. But Hemingway's work easily stands up to such parodies.

3. Emily Dickinson, who spoke as well as wrote in a singularly distinctive voice. This poem does not have Dickinson's idiosyncratic punctuation and capitalization, and so may have been a little harder to identify.

4. From *Dombey and Son* by Charles Dickens. It has the typical Dickens characteristics of a rather loose, accumulating style, with a large number of subordinate clauses.

5. This is Mark Twain's *The Man Who Corrupted Hadleyburg*. The vocabulary is peculiarly Twain's. He used such phrases as "the pandemonium of delight" frequently, and often wrote in an exaggerated and humorous style.

6. Edward Bulwer-Lytton, master of the purple prose, whose works have been parodied widely, wrote *The Last Days of Pompeii*, from which this passage is taken. Lord Bulwer-Lytton's impassioned prose was the basis for the famous "It Was a Dark and Stormy Night" contest, named for the unforgettable first line of this work. This parody contest attracts thousands of entries, including, apparently, one from Snoopy of the Peanuts cartoon series.

7. This is Henry Wadsworth Longfellow using the popular iambic meter: dah-*dah* dah-*dah* dah-*dah* dah-*dah*.

8. Walt Whitman's subject matter and style, blank verse, were extremely unusual in their day. The quotation is from *Leaves of Grass*.

9. Algernon Charles Swinburne, a Victorian poet, was noted for his learned and ornate style. This particularly rich example is from *Ave Atque Vale*.

10. The easily imitated style of Pearl Buck, here represented by a passage from *The Good Earth*, has been the subject of considerable parody. Buck's many books were popular and widely read.

11. Erskine Caldwell, from a short story called "August Afternoon."

12. This is Ogden Nash at his most clever, with his odd but effective rhymes and the unexpectedness of daily trivia contrasted with semiprofound thoughts. This is from *The Face Is Familiar*.

13. From the poem "When All My Five and Country Senses See," by the Welsh poet Dylan Thomas.

14. Jack Kerouac displaying his unique writing style in *On The Road*.

15. This is J. D. Salinger from *Seymour, an Introduction*.

II.

1. c. Virginia Woolf was part of the Bloomsbury Group, so-called because they met at 46 Gordon Square, Bloomsbury (London). The group included Woolf herself, the others listed, and several minor writers of note at that time, including Woolf's sister, Vanessa Bell.

2. e. William Wordsworth moved what was then a great distance to be near Coleridge. Although Wordsworth was very much attached to his sister, Dorothy, she was not a writer. Scott, Coleridge, and DeQuincey were his friends in his professional life.

3. f. Shelley's life was entangled with Byron's in a rather odd way. There was for some time a curious ménage involving Shelley and his wife, and his second wife's half-sister, or stepsister (which she was is not entirely clear), who was romantically involved with Byron.

4. g. Dante Gabriel Rossetti was the leader of the Pre-Raphaelite

Brotherhood, to which the others also belonged. Rossetti wrote, painted, and translated, all in a romantic style.

5. i. Marlowe was such a good friend of Shakespeare's that it is believed he worked with him on *Titus Andronicus,* Shakespeare's first play. Jonson wrote Shakespeare's epitaph.

6. h. Although Lear wrote comic poetry and painted and Coventry Patmore wrote rustic poetry, yet all three were his good friends.

7. j. Nietszche originally admired Wagner for his political views, but they came to a rather abrupt parting of the ways over Wagner's religious beliefs.

8. b. Dreiser was much admired and praised by Mencken and, in England, Arnold Bennett's reviews (and correspondence) were far more favorable than those of the American critics.

9. d. Shaw was a member of the Fabian society for many years. Their socialist-leaning political outlook suited him, and he became friendly with famous socialist and writer Sidney Webb and other members of the society, the name of which comes from Fabius, a Roman general who achieved his ends not by war, but through wariness and caution.

10. a. The three were known as Marxist poets. Day Lewis, incidentally, wrote detective stories under the name of Nicholas Blake, but in his other works he reflects his membership in the Communist Party. (His son, Daniel Day Lewis, has attained a reputation as an actor.)

III.

1. b. FitzGerald's translation of *The Rubaiyát of Omar Khayyám* is the best known of the many translations. It is a free translation, and FitzGerald's rhyme scheme bears no relation to the original.

2. i. The well-known food writer and philosopher on matters gastronomic and otherwise translated Brillat-Savarin fairly recently. *The Physiology of Taste* had been translated previously, but her brilliance and clarity of style made her translation immediately the classic. She combines an inimitable style and a comprehensive knowledge of French culture, cooking, and food.

3. a. Samuel Eliot Morison not only wrote the prize-winning biography of Christopher Columbus, he also translated Columbus's diaries, a major feat.

4. h. Although not the only one, nor the best of the translators, Dorothy Sayers did spend the latter part of her life translating the works of Dante. Sayers was a classical scholar and obviously hoped this would be her masterpiece. It is somewhat ironic that she is better known by far for her Lord Peter Wimsey detective stories.

5. c. Proust was very fortunate in his translator. Most of *Remembrance of Things Past* was translated by Scott-Moncrief. The translation has been considered definitive since it first appeared. Although a new one recently appeared, Scott-Moncrief's translation is still the most often used version.

6. d. H. Wolfe. Anyone who has seen *Cyrano de Bergerac* on the stage or who has read it and has a good ear remembers "Roxane, Roxane, thy name rings in my heart like a silver bell."

7. e. Samuel Beckett, a native English speaker, lived in France for most of his life. He wrote his plays first in French, and then translated them himself into English. He is one of the few native speakers of a language who has been able to learn another language as an adult so successfully as to produce masterpieces in both. Vladimir Nabokov is another, writing in Russian and English, but Joseph Conrad, for example, wrote only in English.

8. f. Constance Garnett, a member of the Bloomsbury Group, and the wife of another famous (at that time) author, Richard Garnett, is renowned for her translations of Russian literature. She produced most of the definitive translations of major Russian writers of her time.

9. g. Chaucer (ca. 1342–1400) translated this collection of stories from the French. His translation became the basis for many subsequent works in English. This translation marks the split from the use of Norman French, as brought to England by William the Conquerer in 1066, and the beginning of the use of everyday English for literature.

10. j. H. T. Lowe-Porter is still the definitive translator of Thomas Mann. She translated nine of Mann's books and those translations are still published today. Several other translators did the remaining five books.

IV.

1. c.	8. m.
2. e. (He was not French, as many think.)	9. l.
	10. d.
3. a.	11. n.
4. k.	12. o.
5. f.	13. g.
6. i.	14. j.
7. h.	15. b.

V.

The code is set to PLUTARCH, and the quote is by Cato, as quoted in Plutarch's Lives.

I WOULD MUCH RATHER HAVE MEN ASK WHY I
HAVE NO STATUE THAN WHY I HAVE ONE.
P L U T A R C H B D E F G I J K M N O Q S V W X Y Z
A B C D E F G H I J K L M N O P Q R S T U V W X Y Z

CHAPTER 10

All Those Words About Literature You Thought You Had Forgotten

This chapter is the grab-bag of all those odd words and facts you ran into in English Lit. 1, or American Lit. 2, or Elizabethan Poets, or some similarly recondite class that made you learn things you would never use again unless you became a writer, an English teacher, an editor, or a trivia buff. Do you remember the types of poetry, the figures of speech, the poetry meters, and what each one means? No? We thought this would probably provide a challenge to your memory.

The following questions provide three possible explanations for each of the words, definitions, or phrases given. All you have to do is identify the correct answer—and recognition is far easier than recall. There is a psychological phenomenon known as the "aha" reaction, which is the shock of recognition that compels one to say "aha." We hope that you will experience that reaction as you recognize the words and phrases you will find, we hope, lurking in the more remote corners of your mind. There are also one or two jokers in the pack.

1. Clerihew
   a. The name of the town in Ireland where George Bernard Shaw was born
   b. A verse form invented by Thomas C. Bentley
   c. A figure of speech that involves comparison of animate and inanimate objects

2. A foot (in poetry)
   a. Three rhyme lines
   b. An accented syllable
   c. A combination of syllables

3. Synecdoche
   a. A figure of speech in which a part stands for a whole
   b. A figure of speech in which exaggeration is the chief characteristic
   c. A form of Greek tragedy

4. Diaeresis
   a. The two small dots over a vowel to show that the adjacent vowels are pronounced
   b. An overblown statement, not necessarily true
   c. The process of exchanging blood through a machine

5. Shakespearean sonnet
   a. A fourteen-line poem rhyming abba abba cde cde
   b. A fourteen-line poem rhyming abab cdcd efgf gg
   c. A fourteen-line poem rhyming abba abba cdc dcd

6. Periphrasis
   a. Wordiness—using many words when one will do

      b. Expressing a thought by means of a paraphrase
      c. A portion of the rostrum in a Roman forum

7. Ellipsis
      a. A literary form that repeats itself circularly
      b. The omission of some words from a sentence
      c. Three periods or asterisks representing something omitted

8. Rondeau
      a. A complicated love plot, in which the characters wind up where they started, like a "round"
      b. A verse form in which a fragment of the first two lines of the first stanza is repeated as a refrain at the end of the second and third stanzas

9. Aldus Manutius
      a. The original form of the word *minuscule,* to mean small.
      b. The first translator of Dante's *Divine Comedy,* often quoted in discussions of the work
      c. The original inventor of the italic form of type and also of the system of punctuation used today

10. Ottavarima
      a. The eight acts of a classical Italian play, derived from Roman tradition
      b. An Italian stanza of eight eleven-syllabled lines or, in its Byronic adaptation of English heroic lines, ten syllables
      c. Any poem of eight verses

11. Euphemism
      a. Using a "nicer" word to blunt an unpleasant idea, like "passed away" for "died"
      b. Expressing oneself in optimistic terms, not always justified
      c. A style of high-flown language popular in the late sixteenth and early seventeenth centuries

12. Aposiopesis
      a. An overblown, exaggerated manner of speaking
      b. The highest form of anything
      c. A figure of speech referring to a speaker who stops as if he cannot remember what he was going to say next

13. Majuscule
    a. A large letter, in type, whether capital or small, but in large type
    b. A type of literary work referring to the Magi, and Biblical themes
    c. The adjective used to refer to authors' major works, rather than their lesser-known works

14. Pleonasm
    a. A name of multiple abnormal growths, derived from "new" and the Greek word for seven
    b. A repetition of words that adds nothing to the sense of the expression
    c. The coining of new words that are made up of parts of other words, like Lewis Carroll's *brillig,* which may be made from *brilliant* and *shining*

15. Acronym
    a. Using the initials of a title or phrase to make a word, like SWAT, which stands for Special Weapons and Tactics
    b. References to anyone or anything by its initials instead of its full name
    c. A style of bitter attack in a speech, with veiled insults

16. Collective nouns
    a. The names of everyone in a group, when all members are listed separately
    b. A generic term for a group of anything
    c. A noun that has come to be made up from various languages, and is thus "collective" as it has collected pieces from its various sources

17. Limerick
    a. A type of poem composed originally in Limerick, Ireland
    b. A nonsense verse in the meter developed by Edward Lear, with the rhyme scheme a a b b a

18. Lipogram
    a. A work written entirely without one or more letters
    b. A diagnostic imaging procedure to measure the amount of

lipids in the blood, i.e., cholesterol (HDL and LDL) or tri-glycerides, and provide a lipid profile

c. Another term for an epigrammatic construction with a witty saying juxtaposed with a rather common proverb

19. Litotes
   a. The use of many adjectives to describe the same thing, as in a "charming, delightful, and thoroughly engaging young lady"
   b. William Joseph Litotes (1747–1794), the famous English revolutionary who went to France as a friend of Danton's and wound up suffering the same fate of being guillotined
   c. An understated way of expressing oneself, as in "the comfortably off King Croesus," in which the adjective is far too modest for the fact

20. Kenning
   a. The Icelandic sagas in non-verse form, as translated into English merely as stories
   b. A form of expression, used often in *Beowulf* and Anglo-Saxon writings, in which a descriptive phrase is used in place of a more well-known word, as "the lamp of heaven" for the sun
   c. The traditional dirge of Celtic peoples over the bodies of slain warriors

ANSWERS

1. b. Thomas Clerihew Bentley, possibly better known as the author of *Trent's Last Case,* also invented the clerihew, a verse form. A typical clever example from his charming book *Biographies for Beginners* is:

    Sir Christopher Wren
    Said "I am going to lunch with some men,
    If anyone calls
    Say I'm designing St. Paul's."

2. b.

3. a. This figure of speech utilizes the part for the whole, as referring to the ocean and the seashore as "the shore."

4. a. This symbol, now scarcely used in English, indicates that two adjoining vowels are pronounced separately. An example would be naive, and another might be reenter. It is still used in French, as for example in the famous French champagne, Moët et Chandon. A similar but not identical symbol exists in German, where it is called an *umlaut.*

5. b. There are two major types of sonnets, Shakespearean and Petrarchan. Examples a and c are typical variations of the Italian form.

6. a. This is sometimes, and more popularly, called pomposity. It involves the use of multisyllabled words, more words than are necessary, and in general a style similar to officialese.

7. b and c. An example of the first might be "the woman he saw" for "the woman whom he saw," where the missing word is easily filled in from the context. The second is often used in partial quotes: This would run ". . . for all practical purposes" when the original had read "It was not necessary, or desirable, to do this, as for all practical purposes, the simpler way was sufficient."

8. b. This charming type of poem is found more in French poetry than in English. In English, its modified version is known as a rondel. Chaucer wrote much of his poetry in this form. A lovely modified form is Leigh Hunt's "Jenny Kissed Me."

9. b and c. Aldus Manutius, or Maniccio, or Manizio, depending upon your encyclopedia, was a fifteenth-century Italian scholar and printer, noted for the accuracy of his work. He published many editions of the classics, in their original Greek or Latin, as scholars of the day could read both. Besides inventing Italic type, he also set up our current system of punctuation. Earlier, it was fairly common to run words together. Manutius used the word breaks, and also a system of punctuation very much like that in use today.

10. b. This is a form of meter with two long syllables. The meter is called heroic, because it was often used in religious invocations. It is most often used in modern poetry—that is, dating back several hundred years—to vary the other meters.

11. a and c. This high-flown, elaborate form of language and writing was taken from John Lyly's work *Euphues, The Anatomy of Wit* (1579), which enjoyed an enormous vogue. Everyone of education tried to use his style in conversation and letters.

12. c. A speaker who interrupts himself with the kind of expression similar to "And as for my worthy opponent . . . but let us return to my original point." The interruption is usually used for the abrupt break of subject, as here.

13. a. The capital letter, as opposed to the lowercase, is not always the sole use. It refers to any large letter, and comes from the Latin *major,* meaning larger.

14. a. "At this point in time" for "now" and "to come to a sudden cessation" for "stop" are examples of pleonasms.

15. a. The proliferation of acronyms seems to be a current fad. Every organization looks for names that can be made into acronyms, apparently on the theory that acronyms are more easily remembered than a multiword title. Many acronyms have supported this theory. Hardly anyone remembers the full names of RADAR or SONAR. The acronyms themselves have become names and nobody ever calls them Radio Detection and Ranging or Sound Navigation and Ranging, even in the most meticulous reporting and writing.

16. b. The collective nouns for many groups are interesting and amusing. James Lipton collected many in his book *An Exaltation of Larks*. After the book came out a favorite game among word fanciers was to make up collective nouns for groups, like a *fold* of maps.

17. b. Edward Lear is the most famous author of limericks. (Isaac Asimov has also written many. A typical limerick was often composed at a party, according to several usually reliable sources, and sung with a refrain of "We'll all go up to Limerick," with no further explanation.) The resulting poem was usually comic and often ribald. Lear did not invent the verse form, although he is sometimes credited, erroneously, with having done so. A typical limerick follows, to illustrate the rhyme scheme and meter:

> As a beauty I'm not a great star
> There are others more handsome by far
> But my face, I don't mind it
> For I am behind it
> It's the folks out in front that I jar.

> —ANTHONY EUWER

(Willard Espy credits Euwer, which is probably correct. The limerick has occasionally been erroneously attributed to Calvin Coolidge, an unlikely story.)

18. a. *Lipogram* is from the Greek and means "lacking a letter." James Thurber wrote a story about a country in which the letter *o* was forbidden. The most famous example of a lipogram is *Gadsby,* written by E. B. White.

19. c. This word is the equivalent of the French, *pas mal*, literally, "not bad," which is used to describe something that is really very good indeed. In English, perhaps, one might say, ". . . no mean actress herself, praised her competitor in the most glowing terms."

20. b. This one keeps coming up whenever *Beowulf* is studied. The Beowulf story uses this figure of speech frequently, "whale path" for ocean, and its use has not died out entirely. A description of a mountain path was referred to in a hiker's magazine as "this ankle-torturer."

Here is a small lagniappe to finish the book—two more quotation puzzles!

To solve a Quotation Puzzle, use the letters at the bottom of each column to fill in the squares at the top of that column. The letters have been arranged alphabetically. A letter will be used once for each time it appears, so cross off each letter as you use it. Black squares indicate word ends. Words may begin on one line and continue on the next.

I.

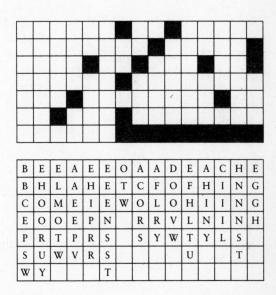

B	E	E	A	E	E	O	A	A	D	E	A	C	H	E
B	H	L	A	H	E	T	C	F	O	F	H	I	N	G
C	O	M	E	I	E	W	O	L	O	H	I	I	N	G
E	O	O	E	P	N		R	R	V	L	N	I	N	H
P	R	T	P	R	S		S	Y	W	T	Y	L	S	
S	U	W	V	R	S				U			T		
W	Y			T										

II.

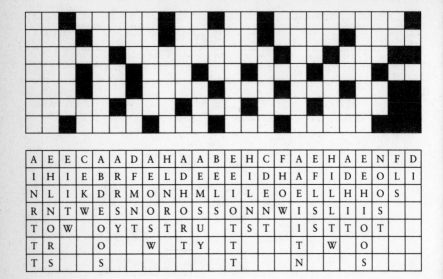

A	E	E	C	A	A	D	A	H	A	A	B	E	H	C	F	A	E	H	A	E	N	F	D
I	H	I	E	B	R	F	E	L	D	E	E	E	I	D	H	A	F	I	D	E	O	L	I
N	L	I	K	D	R	M	O	N	H	M	L	I	L	E	O	E	L	L	H	H	O	S	
R	N	T	W	E	S	N	O	R	O	S	S	O	N	N	W	I	S	L	I	I	S		
T	O	W		O	Y	T	S	T	R	U		T	S	T		I	S	T	T	O	T		
T	R			O			W		T	Y		T				T		W		O			
T	S			S						T				N				S					

ANSWERS

I.

BEWARE OF FALSE PROPHETS WHICH COME TO YOU IN SHEEPS
   CLOTHING BUT INWARDLY THEY ARE RAVENING WOLVES.

II. IN WORDS AS FASHIONS: THE SAME RULES WILL HOLD, / ALIKE
FANTASTIC IF TOO NEW OR OLD, / BE NOT THE FIRST BY / WHOM
THE NEW IS TRIED, / NOR THE LAST TO LAY THE OLD ASIDE.

WHAT IS MENSA?

What is Mensa? It is more than the sum of its parts, that is true. Technically, it is a society spanning more than thirty countries, with a membership, as this is written, of over 100,000. These members share nothing except the bond of having passed an IQ test, properly administered and supervised, at or above the 98th percentile. In other words, these 100,000 score in the top 2 percent of the population worldwide.

The next question is always, What does Mensa do? It is easy to describe members and to say what they don't do: They do not sit around and discuss Einstein's equations. They do not sit around and compare IQ scores. (You can't do that, really, because IQ scores vary from test to test—only percentiles remain unchanged.) They do not agree on many subjects. They do not fit a preconceived mold. They do not all have Ph.D.s. They are not all male or female. They do not all subscribe to the same political philosophy, religion, or even belief in what Mensa can or should do. They are as variegated a group of people as it is possible to find.

In the United States, past and present members include Isaac Asimov, Theodore Bikel, Jean Auel, Donald Peterson, the romance author Rebecca Brandywine, Leslie Charteris (of "The Saint" fame), and many many others, but the ground would be littered with names if we went on. It also includes a post-office employee who is an expert on Victorian England and Sherlock Holmes, and whose lectures on these subjects draw standing-room-only crowds. It includes the British-born engineer whose credits include the gravel island off the North Slope of Alaska where an oil rig was built. She has racked up a list of engineering accomplishments that is indeed impressive. John Ball, the writer, was a member. There are specialists in any field you care to name and also many wide-ranging generalists.

So what actually does go on at meetings? It varies. There are serious discussion groups. There are book-reading and play-reading sessions. There are lunch bunches and so-called Temperance Societies, which meet to discuss the problems of the world. There are usually monthly meetings for each of the 150-plus U.S. groups with, usually, an interesting speaker. There are dinner meetings, full of table hopping and good talk. There are very funny auctions. There are Regional Gatherings, known as RGs, wherein a group of Mensans, numbering anywhere from thirty-five or so to several hundred, gathers at a hotel for a weekend of lectures, games, dances, and parties. There is a Colloquium every other year, with top-notch speakers on subjects such as the future, the gifted child, and the politics of politics. There is the Annual Gathering, or yearly convention, at which up to two thousand Mensans can gather for serious lectures, funny lectures, games, and hospitality. These nonstop get-togethers usually run from Thursday to Sunday night and feature "name" speakers at the banquets, "theme" dances and parties, lectures by experts, and just-plain-fun parties.

You can get out of Mensa whatever you want, but you have to put something in. Mensa has a tiny paid staff. All the rest of the work is done by the Mensans themselves, because they want to do it. If you want a Special Interest Group on Feudal Japan, you start it—as one member did. If you want one on stamp collecting, or paper money collecting, you put a notice in the national magazine, answer all your correspondence, and lo and behold, you have a SIG going. There are several hundred of these specialized groups now, on every imaginable subject and on some that are unimaginable. SIGs are limited only by their founders' imagination and time.

There's a social responsibility side, too. There are scholarships available to non-Mensans. This program has grown from originally offering nine scholarships to offering over fifty today, and many of the local groups award their own. There is a program being run jointly with Montclair State College, in New Jersey, to identify the handicapped gifted. There is also a national gifted children coordinator. There are the awards for excellence, which reward both beginning researchers and those who have been in their field for many years. There is the *Mensa Research Journal*, which reprints award-winning articles on the many aspects of intelligence—intellectual, social, biochemical, and psychobiological. There are the Colloquia. There is the group that has adopted a highway and keeps a section of it clean.

There are many groups working with literacy program volunteers. And there are dozens and dozens more. Again, if you have a pet project, notify the local group and you will probably be able to enlist many, many volunteers. Mensa itself cannot adopt an opinion, but members may support any at all, and often do.

In short, at the present moment, Mensa is 100,000 bright people, enjoying each other's company, all over the world—and any Mensan is welcome at any Mensa meeting anywhere in the world—and cherishing the sense of friendship and fellowship that they find in this unique organization.

Now that you've read about Mensa, and heard about what it is and what it does, why don't you write to:

American Mensa Ltd.
Box LQB
2626 East 14th Street
Brooklyn, New York 11235–3992

In Canada, write to:

Canadian Mensa, Dept. AFS
P.O. Box 505, Station S
Toronto, Ontario M5M 4L8

You will receive information about how to take a standardized test, or which tests you may already have taken that might qualify you for Mensa. You can also obtain an "at-home" test to help you practice on timed tests, if you have not taken such a test in a long time. Information on the various scholarship programs and research awards will also be sent. Some of the scholarships are funded in part by the sale of this book. The sole requirement for joining Mensa is a score at the 98th percentile (the top 2 percent of the population).